GULL LAKE
Yesterday and Today

by
Duane R. Lund
Ph.D.

Distributed by
Adventure Publications, Inc.
P.O. Box 269
Cambridge, MN 55008

ISBN 1-885061-65-X

GULL LAKE
Yesterday and Today

First Printing, 1999
Second Printing, 2001

Printed in the United States of America
by
Nordell Graphic Communications, Inc.
Staples, Minnesota 56479

Dedication

To good friends and mentors:

The late Carl Zapffe, scientist, historian
and author,

and,

The late Pete Humphrey: he knew more
about the culture of American Indians
than anyone I ever met.

I miss them both, very much.

TABLE OF CONTENTS

CHAPTER I
Gull Lake in Prehistoric Times

WHAT MORE CAN A LAKE OFFER?

EITHER YESTERDAY – WITH ITS
- generous supply of fish and wild game,
- nearness to sugar bush forests and wild rice beds,
- and location on the Crow Wing cut-off canoe route with access on the south to the Mississippi River and on the north to the major lakes of what is now Minnesota,

OR TODAY – WITH ITS
- clear, unpolluted waters,
- majestic scenery,
- good fishing,
- extensive opportunity for boat travel and other water sports,
- nearness to full-service communities,
- more than a dozen resorts, some with four seasons of recreational opportunity and,
- several conference centers - among the state's largest and finest.

Surely it is among Minnesota's most historic and enjoyable lakes.

The early maps of what we now call Minnesota identify the lake as "Gayashk", the Ojibwe word for seagull. There is no record of what the Dakotas called the lake when they were here or how it was identified in earlier times.

To learn about prehistoric Gull Lake, we must look to geologists and archeologists.

Geologists tell us that the lake has had its present shape since about 2000 B.C., after the glacial run-off had been completed. It was made considerably larger, however, with the construction of a dam in 1911 on the Gull Lake River outlet just east and south of Gull Point (formerly Squaw Point). The dam raised the lake level about six feet. This gave us a 9,418

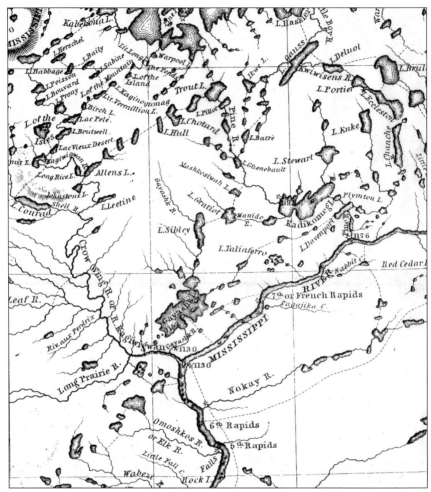

Joseph Nicollet's map of the Gull Lake Region. Gull Lake and River are identified by the Ojibwe name, "Gayashk," meaning seagull.

acre body of water with 38 miles of shoreline (the main lake). If we eliminate all water less than 6 feet deep, we have a good picture of what the lake looked like in prehistoric times. It is likely that many of the village sites are now under water. In fact, Wilson Bay and Steamboat Bay were originally separate lakes.

Lake Agassiz, that gigantic, prehistoric freshwater inland ocean, did not include Gull Lake, but it was less than 100 miles away — to the west and northwest — and probably had considerable impact on the residents of our lake at that time.

Lake Agassiz covered most of what is now northwestern Minnesota and portions of the Dakotas, Manitoba and Ontario. It was larger than all of the Great Lakes combined, including what is now the Red River Valley, the Red Lakes, Lake of the Woods, Lake Winnipeg and Lake Manitoba.

Lake Agassiz was created by the meltdown of the last glacier eight to twelve thousand years ago. (There were probably seven glaciers in all.)

It is truly hard to believe that the Gull Lake area was once covered by glaciers more than one mile thick! There was probably no visible life of any kind on or under the compacted ice and snow. The geography was carved out as the last glacier, called the Pleistocene, moved, grinding boulder against boulder—gouging out the hills and valleys of the landscape. Toward the end, the meltdown was quite rapid and the huge volume of water not only filled the low spots, forming lakes, but also spawned torrential rivers which carved deep channels. The impressive gorges found along the Minnesota and Mississippi Rivers (below where it is joined by the Minnesota) were formed by the gigantic Glacial River Warren.[1]

The drying-up of the huge lake was apparently in stages because ridges which mark the beaches of the receding lake may be seen today from the air or even from some of the highways in the region. Archeologists have discovered village sites on these beaches which would indicate that the earliest people followed the lake north as it dried up.

We know that the first humans to live in the area (including Gull Lake) were contemporary with the animal life of the Ice Age. Ancient burial mounds have been explored which contained ornaments, pottery, tools and weapons made of stone and bone. Some of these artifacts were made of live ivory[2] from the enormous tusks of the woolly mammoth. Since these people were the first inhabitants, at least they did not have to conquer some other tribe in order to move in. They no doubt, however, had their hands full just managing to survive in the hostile environment.

The animal and bird life was very different than today. Not only did the woolly mammoth roam the area but there were varieties of deer (the stag-moose), beaver and bison far larger than the animals we now know. In fact, there were differences even as recently as the coming of the French to this part of North America in the 1600's. Caribou were common then and there were more moose, elk and bear than deer. Passenger pigeons were so numerous it was said that migrating flocks darkened the sky. Today they are extinct.

If geologists are correct in their conclusion that the last of the glaciers receded between eight and twelve thousand years ago, then we can conclude that humans have been in this area a very long time indeed. Perhaps we can better comprehend just how long if we understand that Europeans have been here less than five percent of that human history. Even the Dakota Sioux did not arrive until about 1000 A.D., which represents only about 10 percent of human occupation. Compared to the Dakota Sioux, the Ojibwe were "Johnnies-come-lately", arriving in the 1600's along with the whites. The Ojibwe pushed the Dakota Sioux out of the woodlands of what is now Minnesota and Wisconsin by 1739. It was the beginning of a war that would last more than 100 years.

To give us a better sense of Gull Lake's history, it may help to remember that the historic Ojibwe–Dakota Sioux conflict began before the American Revolution and did not end until during the Civil War, and in all that time the lake was literally caught in the middle of the conflict.

But where did the very early inhabitants of Gull Lake come from? Who were the first to dip their paddles into the cool, clear waters of this lake of lakes?

Archeologists believe that they were descendants of migrants from Asia who had originally crossed to North America by way of the Bering Straits to Alaska. It is thought they then moved down the west coast. From there they migrated east across the continent. One has to wonder why they would leave the pleasant and relatively mild climate of what is now Washington, Oregon and California to travel east over a mountain range, across deep rivers and through a hostile wilderness just to chase a glacier north into the land of woolly mammoths, short face bears and saber-toothed tigers! Were they just curious and wanting to explore? Was there a food shortage? Were they looking for an easier way of life? Or had the west coast become crowded enough so that they decided to find a safer place free from the dangers of attack? The author's guess is "all of the above" with the latter perhaps being the most important reason. Food, however, may have been a problem. We know from oral histories that as recently as a few hundred years ago some tribes became nomadic because of food shortages caused by droughts or because animals upon which they were dependent for food and clothing were becoming scarce. In the 1700's the French recorded times along the present Minnesota-Ontario border when big game and fur bearers died off from disease and/or over-hunting and became critically few in numbers. So it is possible the tribes moved because of a shortage of food.

It is believed that these earliest Native Americans came from a variety of places in Asia[4] because of significant differences among the tribes. Their languages are different; even the root words of tribes that have been in contact for hundreds of years are different. There are also differences in physical appearance. The Dakota Sioux, for example, are relatively tall, while the Ojibwe are of a stockier build. There are also differences in culture including religion, food, pottery, implements, games, etc.

Yet, in spite of these differences, these first peoples had much in common and, indeed, much in common with us. After all, they were human beings, and like us they surely worked for a living, built shelters, clothed themselves according to current styles, played games, developed friendships, laughed, loved, fought, cried, worshipped and cared for their children. They probably lived as families and had special ties with the clans to whom they were related.

We will never know how long the very first inhabitants lived in peace or whether disease claimed them before some other tribe destroyed them, pushed them out, or assimilated them. Surely North America was relatively sparsely populated in those first thousands of years and there should have been room for all. Yet, human nature being what it is, there were no doubt conflicts. "The grass was always greener" elsewhere then, just as it is today and one tribe would no doubt covet another's territory. In the case of America's heartland there was much to covet. The area had both prairie and woodlands where all kinds of animals and birds could be found. Of course, that assumes similarity to the flora and fauna of recorded time. The lakes and streams were probably full of fish.

We do know there was considerable conflict in prehistoric times because large numbers of projectile heads have been found in areas where neither oral nor recorded history tells of battles.

It is not surprising that the farther back in time we go the more difficult it is to find artifacts of those earliest cultures. We do have, however, considerable information about a tribe of people who probably entered our woodlands about the time of Christ. They settled along the Boundary Waters, between Minnesota and Canada and buried their dead in enormous mounds. They are called "the Laurel Culture" and some of the largest mounds are located near Laurel, Minnesota.

The Laurel people may have come from the Pacific Coast or the Gulf of Mexico because shell ornaments have been found in their burial mounds which are of that origin. Their mounds are the largest found in this part of the continent; some are as high as forty feet and over 100 feet in length. There is evidence that these mounds contain the remains of several generations, indicating that these people lived here for quite some time. Other artifacts found in the mounds include sheet copper (probably mined on islands of Lake Superior), decorated pieces of pottery, harpoons, and a variety of projectile heads. The abundance of arrowheads has left archeologists to speculate that these people may have introduced the bow and arrow to this region. It is also of interest that the bones were buried in bundles, indicating that the bodies were probably place in trees or on scaffolds and allowed to decompose before burial. The marrow had been removed from some of the larger bones and the brains removed from some of the skulls shortly after death. In some cases the eye sockets had been filled with clay. Some archeologists have concluded there may have been certain cannibalistic rituals following death. The Laurel people were about the same height as we are today. That is surprising in that we know the human race has grown taller over the years. Soldiers in World War II were taller on the average that their fathers who fought in World War I.

Courtesy Brown's report (Kathio) to the Minnesota Historical Society

Historian J.V. Brower, shown here, describes this mound as approximately 50 feet in length. It is located on Bromley Lake, Aitkin County.

Suits of armor worn by knights in Medieval times would indicate that men were shorter in that day. Interesting that these peoples who lived 2,000 years ago were our size.

Although there is no evidence of these huge mounds in the Gull Lake region, artifacts have been found that may indicate the Laurel peoples moved through this area on their way north and could have lived here for a time, and there are some fairly large mounds in this general area. (see picture). Other huge mounds may be found in Sherburne County by Eagle Lake north of Big Lake and on a bluff overlooking Elk Lake southwest of Princeton.

Some archeologists believe that the earliest mound builders on this part of the continent were the Hopewell Indians of what is now southern Minnesota. Other prehistoric cultures built effigy mounds shaped like animals or birds. White settlers found may of these in Minnesota when they arrived but they have long since fallen victim to the plow.

Sometime around 1000 A.D. a new people arrived in what is now northern Minnesota and Wisconsin and established what has been called the "Blackduck Culture". Whether they pushed the Laural people out or assimilated them is not known, possibly some of each. The Blackduck people buried their dead in pits and then built mounds over the remains. There are many of these mounds in the Gull Lake region.

Some locations on the lake are:

extreme upper end of the lake on the small bay to the east of Spring Creek — 8 mounds,

near both the mouth and source of Gull River,

east side of the long narrows of Upper Gull on the ridge above the marsh – 20 circular mounds, 8 linear mounds,

south end of Upper Gull on a high "island" ridge above the bay near an old railroad bed – 2 mounds and

southeast arm of the southwest portion of Wilson Bay – 2 mounds and possibly some rice pits.

When the second lane was added to Hwy. 371 near where it runs between Gull and Round Lakes, human bones were unearthed.

The Blackduck Culture prevailed in the woodlands until the 1600s when those tribes were pushed out by the Dakota Sioux. This was the first conflict between Native American tribes in this area that we can fairly accurately date.

The Blackduck Culture may have included several tribes, some of which are known today but now live in Manitoba or Ontario.

Oral history tells us that the Assiniboine were chased by their Sioux cousins, the Winnebagos, out of southern Wisconsin. It is thought the Assiniboine originally arrived in Wisconsin from the south or southwest. The Assiniboine were in Minnesota for a time before being pushed north into Ontario and Manitoba by the Dakota Sioux.

According to oral history of the Gros Ventre and the Mandans[5] (they lived along the Missouri River in North Dakota), their forefathers previously lived in what is now Minnesota. The Gros Ventre once showed Ojibwe visitors a map drawn on birchbark which indicated they had once resided on Sandy Lake. Two Canadian Algonquin tribes, the Cree and the Ottawa, lived in northern Minnesota before the Dakota Sioux invasion. The Monsonis (Algonquin-related) were also in the border country during this period. It is not surprising that many of the artifacts that have been found in this region are from the Blackduck Culture. It is believed, for example, that the paintings still visible on the rock cliffs of the Boundary Waters and the Lake of the Woods were the works of the Blackduck Indians.

The Mandans are a particularly interesting people in that they were light complected and some had blond or red hair and blue eyes. Other tribes and early white visitors, such as the La Verendryes, (a family of French-Canadian explorers), concluded they were of European origin or at least had assimilated whites. They even lived in walled villages, some with moats. The houses were arranged as though on streets. According to oral history, they also were Minnesotans for a time and may have been in the central lakes area. Although the Kensington Runestone, which tells the story of Vikings in the Alexandria area (found in the year 1898), has not been accepted as valid by some historians, it is a remarkable coincidence, if nothing else, that this tribe with European blood at one time probably lived in or near that area.

Gull Lake artifacts left behind by the Blackduck Culture include pots and a great abundance of pot fragments. Most of the woodland tribes had elongated pots, in contrast to the rounder pots of the prairie Indians, such as the Dakota Sioux. Remnants of both kinds of pots have been found around Gull Lake.

Although hard evidence is fragmentary, it is possible, and even likely, that all of these tribes we have mentioned visited Gull Lake and may have called it "home" for a time. The reason this is a valid assumption is that the lake was a part of the only north-south canoe route in the woodlands of what is now Minnesota except for the Mississippi River. It was the pre-ferred route when traveling north because there was no current to fight once the canoes entered Gull Lake and it was a little shorter than the Mississippi route. This made traversing the few short portages worthwhile. The route usually followed, after crossing Gull Lake, included Round Lake, Long Lake, Whitefish Lake, Pine River and then a series of small lakes leading to Boy River and then Leech and other northern lakes.

We will discuss in future chapters how the Ojibwe of Gull Lake played very important roles in Native American history as well as in white-Indian relationships in what is now Minnesota. We can probably assume that because of Gull Lake's strategic location, people who lived here before the Ojibwe also had important relationships with others who lived in this region in their time.

Footnotes

[1]For further information, consult *The Historic Upper Mississippi* by this author.

[2]Ivory from the tusks of animals recently killed.

[3]The land masses of North America and Asia are believed to have been joined together at one time.

[4]A small minority of historians speculate that a single tribe may have crossed over from Asia and that the language and other cultural differences came from separation and the passage of thousands of years of time. Others believe the various groups came from as far away as the Mideast and may be some of the lost tribes of Israel. Recent findings indicate at least two major migrations from different origins in Asia.

[5]For more information about the Mandans, consult *The Lake of the Woods, Vol. II, Earliest Accounts*, by this author.

CHAPTER II
The Dakota Sioux and Then the Ojibwe Call Gull Lake Home.

The Dakota Sioux took control of Gull Lake sometime in the early 1600's. As mentioned in the last chapter, archeologists tell us that the Blackduck Indians controlled the woodlands of northern Minnesota including Gull Lake, for several centuries before the coming of the Sioux. It is their best guess that the Blackduck culture was probably dominant from about 1000 A.D. to the coming of the Dakota Sioux to the Minnesota woodlands in the 1600's. The Dakota Sioux were a family of tribes within the Sioux Nation.

THE SIOUX NATION
　　Dakota, Lakota and Nakota[1] (with seven councils)
　　　　Sisseton (Identified with the Nakota)
　　　　Teton
　　　　Yankton
　　　　Yanktonai
　　　　Wahpeton
　　　　Wahpakute
　　　　Mdewakanton
　　Iowa
　　Oto
　　Missouri
　　Omaha
　　Osage
　　Ponca
　　Hidatsa
　　Crow
　　Mandan
　　Assiniboine
　　Winnebago

During the time period that the Blackduck Indians were in the northern woodlands of what is now called Minnesota (1000 A.D. to the 1600's), various Sioux tribes occupied the prairies of the western portion of what we now call the Midwest – including the prairies of western and southern Minnesota. Because the Sioux made such extensive use of the Mississippi and its tributaries, they are sometimes referred to as the "Mississippi Culture." Artifacts lead archeologists to believe that the Dakota Sioux entered the Minnesota prairies about the same time (1000 A.D.) as the Blackduck Indians moved into the northern woodlands. The timing may have been coincidental, or, it is possible the Sioux forced the Blackduck north. After all, we know it was the Dakota Sioux who invaded the woodlands in the 1600's and pushed the Blackducks north into what we now call the "Boundary Waters" and southern Canada.

The stay of the Dakota Sioux in the northern woodlands, including Gull Lake, was relatively brief – probably a little more than 100 years. In 1739, the Ojibwe and their allies, the Cree and Assiniboine in particular, forced the Sioux back south and west onto the prairies.

The Ojibwe as we have already mentioned are relative newcomers to this part of the continent. They are a member of the Algonquin Nation.

THE ALGONQUIN NATION

Ojibwe (also called Chippewa or Anishinaubay)[2]
Ottawa
Sac
Fox
Potawatomi
Illinois
Shawnee
Miami
Kickapoo
Menominees
Cree

In 1600, the Algonquin tribes occupied the eastern portion of the Midwest, with the Ojibwe as far east as New England. They were neighbors of the hostile Iroquois family of tribes.

The Iroquois were among the first to acquire guns from the early white colonists and with this tremendous advantage drove the Ojibwe west on both sides (north and south) of the Great Lakes. Some sources claim that upwards of 10,000 Ojibwe were killed in the process. During the 1600's, the Ojibwe came far enough west to occupy what is now Wisconsin and an area north of Lake Superior, thus becoming neighbors to the Dakota Sioux.

As white explorers, accompanied by their priests, ventured westward they found the Ojibwe scattered over a large area, both north and south of Lake Superior. When missionaries arrived at Sault Ste. Marie in 1640, they found a sizable concentration of Ojibwe. This village grew to an estimated population of 2000 by 1680–a virtual metropolis by the standards of the northern tribes. After 1680 the Ojibwe moved farther west and the village declined in both size and importance. A new concentration developed at La Point[3] – on Madeline Island at the mouth of Chequamegon Bay on Lake Superior. This new capital of the Ojibwe Nation eventually had a population of about 1,000.

The Ojibwe migration routes lead both north and south of Lake Superior; the majority chose the southern route and settled in Wisconsin. Those using the northern way settled along the north shore of Lake Superior and around Rainy Lake and Lake of the Woods. Contrary to what we might expect, there was little confrontation at first between the Ojibwe and the Sioux. The basic reason was economic. The French needed the furs of the Minnesota Lake region and knew virtually none would be available if the Sioux and Ojibwe were at war. The Sioux and the Ojibwe realized too that there would be no trade items available to them if they had to spend their time defending themselves against an enemy instead of collecting furs.

Du Luth was the chief negotiator and genuine hero of the peace-keeping effort. He wintered with the Ojibwe at Sault Ste. Marie in 1678-79 and during that time developed a good working relationship with both the French traders and the Indians. With the coming of the ice break-up in the spring, Du Luth led a band of Ojibwe to a site near the city which now bears his name, and there held a council with several tribes in an attempt to expand the fur trade industry into Minnesota and southern Ontario. At this meeting, representatives of the Dakota, Cree, and Assiniboine pledged friendship and cooperation with the French and Ojibwe. No mean accomplishment. Because there were so few French traders, the Ojibwe were to serve as middlemen, representing the French in trading with the Sioux and other tribes. It worked for about 60 years. Du Luth also used the occasion to lay claim to the entire upper Mississippi area for France. In the same year (1679), Du Luth founded a trading post at Grand Portage on Lake Superior. From this base he established trade with the Sioux tribes of the lake region with the Ojibwe as the traders. Grand Portage was destined to become the rendezvous point for the voyageurs from Montreal ("porkeaters") and those from Lake Athabasca and other western points ("men of the north"). Because it was impossible to travel all the way from Montreal to the trading posts in the west and return in a single season, a meeting place was necessary for the exchange of furs and trade goods. Grand Portage was that place. This rendezvous, in July of each year, was an occasion for great celebration.

Trade developed rapidly. LaSalle reported in 1682 that the Ojibwe were trading with the Dakotas as far as 150 miles to the west of the Mississippi.

The peaceful arrangement allowed large numbers of Ojibwe to settle in Wisconsin and along both the north and south shores of Lake Superior. But the peace was too good to last. The Sioux of the prairies (Lakota and Nakota) had not been included in Du Luth's conference and they frequently sent raiding parties into the Boundary Waters. By 1730 the truce was an uneasy one.

It was this testy atmosphere that greeted the French-Canadian explorer, Pierre La Verendrye, upon his arrival at Lake of the Woods in 1732. His construction of Fort St. Charles on the Northwest Angle of that lake helped keep the peace for a time, but the warpath which led from the plains of the Dakota to its terminal point at present day Warroad, on Lake of the Woods, was once again in use. La Verendrye, like other Frenchmen, allied himself with the Ojibwe, Cree and Assiniboine. It is not surprising, therefore, that the Sioux of the prairies eventually launched a direct attack on the French. The Lakota[4] massacre on Lake of the Woods of twenty-one Frenchmen—including La Verendrye's eldest son, Jean Baptiste, and his priest, Father Alneau—really marked the beginning of all-out war between the Dakotas and the Ojibwe and their allies, the Crees and the Assiniboines. In the same year (1736) the Ojibwe gained a measure of revenge for La Verendrye by launching a raiding party from La Pointe into southeastern Minnesota. The Cree, Assiniboine and some Ojibwe had begged La Verendrye to lead an attack against the Sioux, but in his wisdom he refused. He knew that open warfare would bring more Sioux to that area and could very well mean the end for sometime to the fur trade business. His entire expedition was financed by Montreal merchants who had been growing more and more demanding for a better return on their investment. Without furs there would be no support from the East.

La Verendrye reminded the Cree, Assiniboine, Monsonis and the Ojibwe that it was the Lakota Sioux from the prairies, not the Dakota Sioux of the woodlands, who killed his men. He addressed the Ojibwe in particular, pointing out the good relations they had developed with the Dakota Sioux as they brought them trading goods in exchange for furs. La Verendrye made it clear to all tribes that the French had no quarrel with the Sioux of the woodlands. His efforts were in vain as raiding parties were sent against the Dakota Sioux from what is now Canada and western Wisconsin. Within three short years after the Lake of the Woods massacre, the Dakota Sioux were dislodged from all of their Minnesota woodlands strongholds, including Gull Lake.

The first attacks on the woodland lakes of what is now Minnesota were not by the Ojibwe, but by their allies the Crees and Assiniboines from the north. Launching their attack from their Lake of the Woods and boundary water villages, they drove down on the Red Lakes, Winnibigoshish,

Cass and then Leech. The Ojibwe seemed almost reluctant at first to join battle. Perhaps it was because their leadership still felt a loyalty to the French and their pursuit of peace among the tribes. However, when they had once committed themselves, it was with a vengeance. The Dakota villages at Sandy Lake were among the first to fall to the Ojibwe and their allies – and this site was to become the new capital of the Ojibwe Nation. Located on the watershed between Lake Superior and the Mississippi lake region at the end of the Savanna portage, it was the key to control of the entire area. The Cree were perhaps the first to establish villages on Leech Lake following the rout of the Sioux.

Thus, by 1739, the Dakotas had fled from their lake area strongholds and had moved their families to the prairies, and back into the southern part of the state – particularly along the Minnesota River. The once powerful Mille Lacs village of Kathio – what was left of it – was moved to the mouth of the Rum River. But the war was by no means over. It was really the beginning of a hundred year's war. No sooner would the Sioux be driven from an area than they would plan a counterattack. If the Ojibwe or their allies moved out of an area, the Dakotas moved back in. Sometimes old village sites were even resettled by the original Sioux families. Although the Dakotas had been driven from their strongholds, they certainly had not given up; nor were the Ojibwe and their allies strong enough to occupy and control the area. When villages were first established by the Ojibwe and their allies, they were often wiped out – including women and children. All of northern Minnesota soon became a virtual "no man's land" inhabited mostly by marauding war parties. The bands were not large – usually less than 100 braves in number. From 1739 to 1766, few tried to "live" in the area, and all who entered did so with intent to wage war. But when the ice went out of the lakes in the spring of 1766, the Ojibwe organized an army of about 400 warriors from their villages along Lake Superior and throughout Wisconsin. When the war party left Fond du Lac it was said that a man standing on a high hill could not see the end or the beginning of the line formed by the Indians walking in single file – as was their custom.

By mid-May, the better-armed Ojibwe had met and soundly defeated a much larger "army" of Dakotas, perhaps as many as 600 braves. The Dakotas at first fell back to Leech Lake and solidified their forces. Their first strategy was to occupy the islands of the lake. If they had been content to wait it out here until reinforcements arrived, they would have been relatively safe and could have held out for some time. However, over eager and, over confident, the Dakotas made a grave error in strategy. They divided their forces and launched three simultaneous attacks on Pembina, Rainy Lake and Sandy Lake. They lost on all three fronts and the resultant disaster was the turning point of the war. The Sioux fell back to their

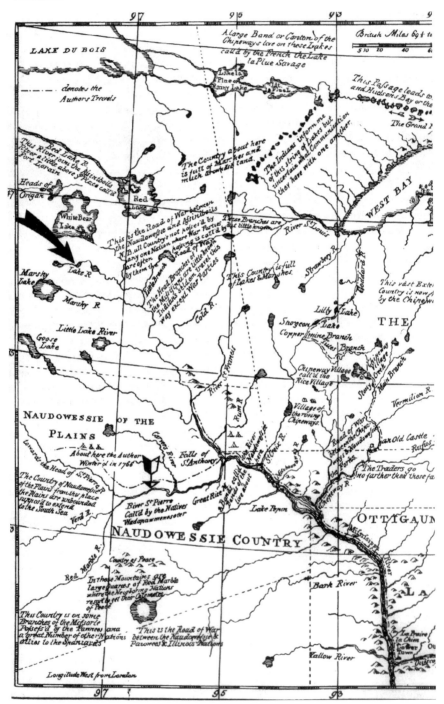

Jonathan Carver's Map – based on his explorations in 1766 and 1767. The large black arrow near the left margin marks the Crow Wing River. He calls it "Lake River".

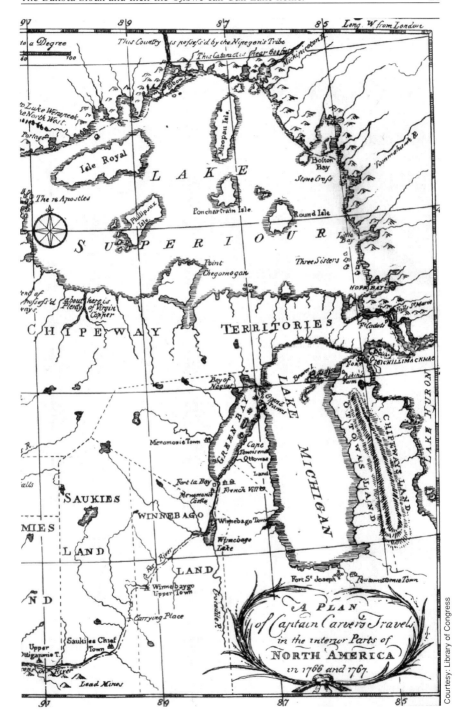

OJIBWE LODGE   *SIOUX TEEPEE*

In winter, two layers of hides and/or bark were used to provide insulation.

villages west of the Mississippi and along the Minnesota River but they were able to keep their stronghold on the Mississippi at the mouth of the Rum River.

The Ojibwe were for the first time truly in control of the lake region and a serious effort was made to settle the area. Sandy Lake continued as the headquarters for their operations but villages soon appeared on the Red Lakes, Winnibigoshish, Cass Lake, Leech Lake, Gull Lake and Mille Lacs. Even though the Ojibwe had effectively defeated the Dakotas, Sioux war parties would return again and again for many years to view their old village sites, visit the burial places of their ancestors, and administer vengeance to the Ojibwe. In fact, if the Ojibwe villages had not been replenished continuously with settlers from the east, they surely would have been annihilated.

We shall see in the next chapter how the fighting continued, with few interruptions, for more than 100 years – up to the time of the Civil War (1862).

Because the Dakota Sioux and the Ojibwe have played such important roles in the history of Gull Lake, it is appropriate that before going on we take a closer look at the two cultures.

First, let us generalize that the people of these two great tribes were far more alike than they were different. Both, while in Minnesota, were dependent upon the woods, lakes, prairies, and streams for survival. The trees, especially the birch, furnished materials for both shelter and transportation. Animal life provided meat and clothing. Bones were used for tools and hooks. Fish and fowl made for the finest of eating. The berries and nuts of the woods and the wild rice of the lakes and streams were also important foods. Stones were shaped into both tools and weapons. Before the coming of guns and powder, both peoples used spears and bows and arrows. Clay soil was used to fashion pottery and utensils. With the coming of the trader, all sorts of ironware, knives and trinkets became available. Metal soon replaced stone for arrowheads and was also used in other weapons. Indians took well to gardening. Pierre La Verendrye taught them how on Lake of the Woods in the 1730's and Simon Dawson, in 1857, was astounded to find an eight acre garden on an island in the Northwest Angle. Other tribes learned gardening on their own or from other tribes. Most of what the Indian took from his environment was for survival, but he did harvest one luxury — tobacco. In Minnesota, the chief ingredient came from the dried inner bark of the kinnikinic (red willow) which was often mixed with powdered leaves and roots from other plants. In the prairies, the wild tobacco plant was used by the various Sioux tribes. Pipes made from stone (catlinite)[5] taken from the quarries near Pipestone, Minnesota, were used by many tribes — often long distances from this source. Smoking also marked ceremonial occasions, much as toasting with alcoholic drinks has been customary for centuries on special occasions in other civilizations. The pipe also was (and is) an impor-

Syrup was made by boiling sap for days over an open fire.

tant part of worship. Smoke, like incense in other cultures, represents prayers to the Supreme Being.

Both tribes loved paint and feathers. Both were a singing and dancing people. They were gregarious and lovers of feasts and games. The Sioux particularly enjoyed "betting."

There were few differences in how the Sioux and Ojibwe made use of nature's bounty while residing in our state. Both, for example, harvested the sap from the maple tree and used it to make sugar. In late March or early April, the return of the first crow caused great rejoicing because it signaled the coming of spring and the rising of the sap in the maple trees. Winter hunting encampments would break up. The Crow Wing and the Long Prairie Rivers were favorite wintering locations for the Leech Lake, Sand Lake, Gull Lake and Mille Lacs Lakes Ojibwe. The tribes from the north usually returned through Gull Lake on their way home from the Crow Wing and Long Prairie Rivers. The families, relations and even whole villages would move to their traditional "sugar bush" area where they would stay until May. Permanent lodges were located at these sites. They were large, usually measuring from 10 to 20 feet wide and 25 to 40 feet long. Sometimes smaller, temporary huts were built – called "wig-wa-si-ga-mig" by the Ojibwe. Whites nicknamed them "wigwams." The trees were tapped by cutting a slash and driving a cedar splinter or carved spigot into the wood. The sap dripped off the splinter and was then collected

Ojibwe Scalp dance–from watercolor by Peter Rindisbacker in West Point Museum. White explorers were impressed with the muscular physique of Native Americans, early drawings made them look like Greek Athletes!

in containers on the ground (made from birchbark). Syrup was made by boiling the sap for days over an open fire. Although the syrup was sometimes used for food, it was usually thickened by continued boiling and then when it was the right consistency, placed in a basswood trough where it was gently stirred until it became granulated, thus forming sugar. Before there were iron kettles, birch bark containers held the sap and hot stones were dropped into the liquid.

Often times the syrup was poured into molds and allowed to harden. This "hard sugar" could be stored more conveniently for use throughout the year. One family could prepare as much as 500 pounds of maple sugar in a single season. The hard sugar was eaten as a food or confection; granulated sugar was used as a seasoning or flavoring agent; and a beverage was made by dissolving the maple sugar in water.

There were large groves of maple trees in the Gull Lake area, particularly east of the lake.

Spring was also the time for fishing, trapping and hunting. In addition to using nets and traps, spawning fish were often speared at night with a birch bark or pine knot torch for light. Migratory waterfowl were again found on the Indian menu. Muskrats and beaver were easier to trap. All in all, spring was a time for both work and rejoicing. Celebrations, feasting and religious ceremonies accompanied the spring activities.

July and August were a season for berry picking. The braves may have been helpful in locating the berry patches, but the women and children did the picking. Just as today, the woodlands had an abundance of blueberries, chokecherries, pincherries, raspberries, strawberries, and cranberries (both low and high bush). Every effort was made to preserve the fruit for use later in the year. Some berries were dried whole; others were dried and then pulverized. Boiling was sometimes used, particularly with raspberries. Pemmican, a Sioux favorite, was made by mixing dried berries with animal fat and stuffing the mixture into animal intestine casings. It was also at this time that ducks and geese became quite helpless during a period of molting and young birds were taken just before they were large enough to fly. Unsportsmanlike? Not when you're talking about food for survival!

September brought the wild rice harvest and another occasion to feast and celebrate. It was perhaps even a greater time for reunions and socializing than the sugar camps. Most harvesting was done by the women, usually two to a canoe. While one paddled or poled the boat through the rice bed, the other sat in front and pulled the rice over the canoe, beating the heads with a stick — thus dislodging the mature kernels. Since all of the rice in each head did not mature at the same time, the harvesters could cover the same area several times a few days apart.

The kernels were further separated from the husks by beating or trampling and then the chaff was blown away by throwing the rice into the air on a windy day. The kernels were then parched by the fire.

The same animals that are found in Minnesota today were here centuries ago — plus a few more. Buffalo, caribou and elk were common in Minnesota — even after white men first arrived. Most animals, such as moose, were probably more plentiful than today, but others, such as deer, may have been less plentiful. But for all of the animal life, hunting was not always easy. Such primitive weapons as spears and bows and arrows gave wild game a great advantage. Predators and disease probably took a greater toll than the Indians, and severe winters were hard on both the hunter and the hunted.

Although there were few differences in how the Ojibwe and the Dakotas made use of nature's bounty, in some ways the tribes were not alike. Language was perhaps the most significant difference. Even though

Courtesy of the Beltrami County Historical Society

Chief Bemidji. He was not really a chief but was well liked and highly respected by all. He lived where the Mississippi enters Lake Bemidji. The word "Bemidji" is an Ojibwe word meaning "a lake that has a river running through it."

several tribes of the Algonquins and the Sioux had been neighbors for centuries, even the basic root words bore no resemblance. It is likely that the ancestors of these two tribes migrated to North America at different periods of history and from different parts of Asia. Differences in facial and other physical characteristics were accented by diverse clothing, head gear, and hair styles. As mentioned earlier, the Sioux were of a tall but athletic build, while the Ojibwe were more stocky but sturdy. White explorers were impressed with the muscular physique of the Native Americans; early drawings made them look like Greek athletes!

Both tribes were very religious, but there were significant differences as well as similarities.

Both believed in a Supreme Being or Great Spirit. Both believed in a life after death. Both had a multitude of lesser gods or spirits — usually taken from nature. The Sioux labeled the spirits or the unknown as "waken;" The Ojibwe called them "manitou." Religion called for such virtues as patience, truth and honesty, but curses were called down upon enemies. Superstitions and religious legends were numerous and varied somewhat from tribe to tribe and village to village. Gods were worshipped in prayers, offerings, chants and dances. The Ojibwe in particular, were conscientious about offering prayers whenever food was harvested or taken in a hunt. Visions and dreams were generated by fasting and meditation. Tobacco was often offered as a sacrifice.

"The happy hunting ground" was a place where the Indian was free from his struggle for survival and all the necessities of life were easily attained. Chief Bemidji described the Indian's "Hell" as a place where the hungry Indian could see hundreds of walleyes through six feet of ice with no way to cut through, or a deer was always just going over the second hill as he came over the first, or he was very cold and all the wood was too wet to start a fire.

Medicine men were both priests and healers. When herbs or other medicines did not work they exorcised evil spirits. They practiced the "laying

Courtesy of Carl Zapffe.

Ojibwe "spirit houses" over graves.

on of hands" to invoke a blessing.

The help of the gods was sought before each serious endeavor, whether it be waging war, hunting or whatever.

Dances often included a religious or other serious purpose and were not just for entertainment.

The Ojibwe had a religious-cultural hero named "Nanabozho," who created the world for the Indian and taught him about the Great Spirit and religious practices. The practices were called "Midewiwin," and they were characterized by secret ceremonies and initiations including a guardian spirit for each and a "totem" spirit for each family group or relation. The Ojibwe had about twenty totems with as many as 1,000 members in a totem family. It was taboo for members of the same totem to marry. There were a few examples of the totem practice among Sioux tribes but it is believed that these can be traced in each case to intermarriages with the Ojibwe. The totem was symbolized by a bird, animal, reptile or fish. In addition, each Ojibwe carried a medicine bag which contained herbs and items such as shells which represented special powers and protection. The priests were called "Mides."

Polygamy was permitted by both tribes with the male taking more than one wife. Because so many men were killed in battle, this was necessary to maintain the population.

Upon death, following a ceremony and appropriate mourning[6], bodies were sometimes bundled on scaffolds or placed in trees – particularly during the cold time of the year – and buried later. The Ojibwe traditionally buried their dead in a sitting position facing west. A long, low house-like shelter was constructed over the grave. Food was placed here along with all the deceased would need in the way of tools and weapons to help in the journey westward "across the river" to an eternal reward. A carved or drawn symbol of the appropriate totem was often placed outside the shelter.

In the novel "White Indian Boy[7]" by this author, we are given a look at a Midewiwin ceremony of the Ojibwe through the eyes of young Johnny

Ojibwe mourners and spirit houses.

A Midewiwin Lodge

Tanner, hero of the book:

In the years to come, Johnny would have many pleasant memories associated with the months the family would spend at Rainy Lake and over those years he would return again and again to visit the village. Among the more interesting of those memories would be his exposure to several new facets of Ojibwe religion and tradition.

Shortly after Net-no-kwa (Johnny's mother) and the boys arrived at the village, the very secret and mysterious Midewinin ceremony was held. The ever-curious Johnny heard about the preparations and had many questions for his new brother-in-law, beginning with "What is the purpose of the ceremony? Is it something a person belongs to?"

"Whoa, Little Falcon[8] — one question at a time." Maji-go-bo replied. "Yes, it is a secret society people belong to, but because it is secret there isn't a great deal I am permitted to tell you. However, it is common knowledge among all Indians that its purpose is to help its members stay in good health, heal them when they are sick, and make it possible for them to enjoy long life."

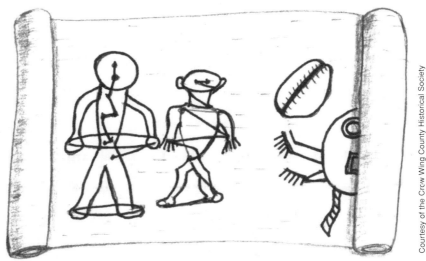

Courtesy of the Crow Wing County Historical Society

A birch scroll depicting the Midewiwin ceremony. Note the clam shell right of center. The clam was an important Ojibwe symbol. Some believe its significance can be trace to the generations of Ojibwe who lived by the Atlantic Ocean. Some current scholars also suggest that as the tribes followed the receding glaciers north, the ice cap in the distance may have resembled a clam.

"Are you a member, Maji-go-bo?"

"Yes, I was initiated several years ago."

"Can anybody join?" Johnny asked.

"I guess so, but you must ask to be admitted. One becomes eligible to apply if he is healed by a member of the society or if he has a vision or a dream in which the Great Spirit makes it clear that he should seek membership."

"Is the chief the leader?" was the next question.

"No, the society is run by the medicine men; they are called "Mides". You will be allowed to witness the ceremonies and the Mides will be the ones who direct the proceedings."

At this point Maji-go-bo stopped talking, so Johnny prodded him with, "Tell me more."

"There really isn't much more I am allowed to tell you, except, maybe, that there are "degrees" of accomplishment or honors one may attain— four of them in all—but I cannot tell you anything more about them. I understand other lodges have eight degrees and it is said degrees are sometimes taught beyond the customary four or eight, but those often teach black magic. Some of these evil Mides who teach additional degrees are called "Bear Walkers" because they are said to go about at night disguised in a bear skin taking vengeance on their enemies."

Johnny's curiosity was really piqued by this time, but he knew it would be improper to pursue the inquiry further.

On the first day of the ceremony Maji-go-bo took Wa-me-gon-a-biew, (Johnny's Indian brother) and Johnny with him to witness the big event. As they drew near the far side of the village, Johnny was surprised to see an enormous lodge, about 200 feet long, approximately 30 feet wide, and maybe 10 feet high. It was constructed in the same manner as the lodges the Indians lived in, with the larger end of small trees set into the ground and the tops bent over and lashed together in the middle. But just the framework was there, there was no hide or bark covering and the spectators could see all that went on inside. However, only the members or those about to join were admitted into the enclosure.

As the participants arrived, some carried drums of skin stretched over hollow sections of logs or across a wooden circular frame, others carried rattles. Many had pipes, and still others carried what looked like scrolls of birchbark. "What do you suppose those birchbark rolls are for?" Johnny asked his brother.

"I don't know but I understand there are pictures and symbols written on them that have some magical meaning," Wa-me-gon-a-biew replied.

The initiates stood in a separate group as they arrived, but before they were allowed to enter the big lodge they had to first take a steam bath in a small hut close to the lake as sort of a purification ceremony. Water was splashed on very hot rocks and the people stayed inside as long as they could stand the steam. When they could take no more they would dash to the water's edge and dive in.

Noticing that some were very young, Johnny asked Wa-me-gon-a-biew, "Why don't you belong to the lodge?"

"Midewinin practices were not common where we used to live," he replied.

The purging completed, the initiates approached the enclosure and the ceremony commenced. Those who were already members were the first to enter the lodge—following the medicine men, and led by the chief priest. Each initiate brought a dead dog which he lay in front of the entrance and which he had to step over as he entered the lodge. The dogs would later be roasted and eaten during the ceremony. As a part of the ritual, present lodge members stood around the doorway and *tried to dissuade the new members from entering. However, each initiate looked neither to the right nor to the left but kept his eyes straight ahead on the medicine pole which had been erected as the focal point in the enclosure. The new members also carried gifts for the Mides; the higher the degree they were seeking, the more valuable the gift. The hundred or more occupants of the lodge followed the leadership of the priests—dancing, singing, shaking their rattles, beating their drums and repeating secret words and phrases as they paraded around the inside of the enclosure. After more than an hour of these preliminary activities, everyone sat down in their previously assigned positions. Later in the day the new members were initiated.*

For the boys, the most intriguing part of the ceremony was when the Mides pretended to shoot snail and clam shells into the bodies of the new members. Each pretended to be struck down as though dead but then with the encouragement of the medicine men made believe they were coughing up the shells into their hands. These shells were supposed to have great magical and protective powers and were placed in their medicine pouches for safe keeping.

In the same book, *"White Indian Boy"*, Johnny experiences the traditional Ojibwe ritual through which a boy enters manhood:

Net-no-kwa, Johnny's Indian mother, made the arrangements and a few days hence Maji-go-bo, Johnny's' brother-in-law, huddled with his new protégé. He explained the rules. First he must blacken his face with charcoal, and then spend 10 days alone in the bush without eating or speaking to anyone he might chance to see. "And you must pray each day," he added, "petitioning the Great Spirit to show you your guardian spirit through a vision or a dream."

"This is a good time to ask me any other questions you would ask your father if he were here, about Indian ways or about growing into being a brave."

Never short on words, Johnny responded with a barrage of questions as though he might never again have the opportunity to ask an adult about anything. Only bedtime and complete weariness on Johnny's part saved Maji-go-bo from the marathon of inquiries.

After a day of stuffing himself with food almost to the point of becoming ill, Johnny took to the woods. The first three days were uneventful— but miserable. Johnny was tempted to eat even the buds on the trees, but he held firm to his commitment. By the third day, water seemed to satisfy his hunger pangs. He slept as much as he could, thus helping the time to pass and at the same time conserving his strength. The nights were the toughest. Johnny had never heard so many night sounds. He didn't mind the loons on the far off lake or the owls up in the tree tops, but raccoons, deer and other night creatures made suspicious noises as they moved through the dry leaves still on the ground from the previous autumn. At night a boy's imagination works overtime and he thought every raccoon was a skunk and every deer a lynx.

On the sixth morning, Johnny walked down to a stream for a drink of water, but found someone there before him—a cow moose and her twin calves. They had not noticed his approach so he clapped his hands and shouted expecting the clumsy calves to fall over each other trying to escape. To his surprise all three just stared at him. When the mother located the source of the disturbance she shook her big head and pawed the shallow water where she stood, throwing mud and rocks into the brush behind her. That was enough for Johnny and he took off into the woods, but he could hear the monstrous animal in pursuit. He knew he couldn't outrun her so he stopped behind a substantial clump of birch trees. Mother moose had no hesitation in playing a game of "round the birches." A couple of times she reared up on her hind legs like a horse as though to trample her young adversary. In Johnny's weakened condition he knew he couldn't keep this up much longer so he scampered up the largest of the trees. When the moose understood his move she gave him a boost with her nose—but the help was purely accidental; she really didn't want him out of her reach. The huge beast continued to make threatening motions with her head and hooves, but Johnny was safely out of harm's way. Just when she seemed to be calming down, the calves showed up and she again worked herself into a frenzy. After what seemed like hours the moose gave up and led her calves away.

When Johnny was sure he was safe he crawled down and stretched. Then, as though she had been waiting in ambush, the moose thundered back on the scene. Johnny retreated up the tree, and none too soon. And so there was a repeat performance of pawing and head shaking and brushing against the clump of trees. She didn't stay nearly as long as the first time, but again when Johnny descended she was back. This time he had kept one hand on a substantial branch and the moose wasn't even close by the time he was 10 feet up in the air. Apparently the animal's anger and frustration finally turned to discouragement because this time she left for good. Johnny spent the rest of the day very close to trees he could climb and come dark he built himself a cradle like platform in another clump of birches. There was no way he would sleep on the ground with the moose and her calves in the vicinity!

Before going to sleep, Johnny again prayed that he could be given a guardian spirit. As he finally dozed off he was thinking, "It would be just my luck to dream about a moose; after all the trouble they've given me I don't think I could trust a moose spirit to be on my side."

Shortly after he fell asleep, Johnny moved just right—or just wrong— and awoke with a crash as he landed on the ground flat on his back! He was sure the moose had him. But when there was no attack he finally figured out what had happened and crawled back up to his cradle. This time it was nearly daybreak when he finally dozed off once again. As the sun rose he was still fast asleep. A crow alighted in his tree and began an awful racket—all of which triggered a dream in Johnny's tired brain. He thought he had once again fallen to the ground and the moose calves were attacking him. In his dream he heard crows cawing and imagined that dozens of the big black birds drove off the moose calves and carried him with their beaks to the top of a big pine tree and safety. Then he dreamed he was falling....falling...falling down through the branches; as he regained consciousness he realized he actually was falling! But this time he was awake enough to grab at the branches as they passed by and broke his fall, actually landing on his feet. As he stood there, leaning against a tree trunk for support and trying to catch his breath, he suddenly realized, "Hey! I've had my dream! The crow is my guardian spirit!"

All that day Johnny searched for a crow feather to put in the deerskin medicine pouch Net-no-kwa had given him before he left the village. He saw several crows' nests but no feathers were to be found on the ground below. Then he had an idea, why not climb one of those trees? There would surely be some feathers in a nest. He retraced his steps to the last one he had seen—in a huge Norway pine with the nest well up towards the top. After resting a considerable time to regain his strength, he began the climb. The possibility of young ones being in the nest had never occurred to him. About half way up an adult crow discovered him and cried out in alarm. Crows came from every where—dozens of them. Their cawing was deafening as they took turns diving at Johnny, coming so close he could easily have hit or kicked several, but he just held on for dear life. Suddenly one of the crows landed in the nest, killed the half grown young one that was there, and pushed it out! The fluttering of the dead bird to the ground was like a signal. The cawing ceased and every crow flew away. Almost sadly, Johnny slid down and picked up the dead bird. Staring at the lifeless form he rationalized, "Maybe it was meant to be."

Anyway, the quest was over. Taking his knife from his belt, Johnny cut off one claw. Then he plucked the longest feather from a wing, and placed both items in his medicine pouch. He was a brave!

In his book, *"Indian Days"* the late Carl Zapffe, scientist and historian, gives the following description of the powers of a "jeesaki" (the name given leading medicine men who were also prophets):

We can take a quick look at one of the numerous published descriptions of awe-inspiring Jeesaki ceremonies which should at least settle the claim that the phenomena are real, not fraudulent, and thus far beyond scientific explanation. The record appears in a publication of the Smithsonian Institution. The time: 1858; place: Leech Lake; and the purpose in this case was not to secure other world aid for some situation of human need, but this time simply to prove other-world intervention as factual. On the other hand, perhaps this can be classed as a human need.

Be that as it may, the widely renowned Government Interpreter Paul Beaulieu, it seems, had challenged a local Jeesaki, placing $100 on a wager that the man could not perform to the satisfaction of himself and a committee of twelve men including the resident Episcopal clergyman. Beaulieu prepared a list of several "crucial tests" allowing the Jeesaki to select any one of them that he wished. Which he did.

Poles were cut, sunk deeply into the ground, and on a slant allowing about a 10-inch hole at the top for "Spirit entry". Cross staves were then lashed to the frame to make the special kind of shelter called a Jeesakan; and this was then completely covered with blankets and birchbark except for a tiny flap door, so small that no man could get in or out without assistance. The Jeesaki was tied with a strong rope, and by Beaulieu himself, who began by pulling a tight knot around his ankles, next winding the rope behind the knees and forward to tie both wrists. Laying the man's arms atop his bent knees, he then passed a billet of wood through the gap between the backside of the knees and the foreside of his elbows; roped all of this to the knees and arms while making four passes around his neck; then pulled on it until agreement on the part of the committee was unanimous that the man could never possibly escape — no way! Even the several hundred onlookers thought it a bit overdone. The only way they could get him into the shelter was to lay the man on a small mat and push him through the little doorway. Meantime no objections were raised by the Jeesaki to any of this, though he did enter one request: He needed his Sacred Pipe and Sacred Stone with him — a polished chunk of black basalt. Would they please slide them beneath his body before closing the flap?

This they did. His chants and prayers began; and almost immediately there were loud thumping noises; several voices could be heard inside; none in a recognizable language; the Jeesakan began swaying with rapidly increasing violence — and the Episcopal Priest quickly got the Hell out of there! Forgetting the glossolalia and related phenomena in his own church history, this man was now fully convinced that Satan was behind it all, and that "this was not the place for him!"

Scarcely had he cleared the site, however, and retreated over the hill, when the ruckus began calming down. Then a voice was heard which clearly did belong to the Jeesaki:

"Mr. Beaulieu, go to your home and get your rope!"

Since every care had been taken to protect such things even as confederacy between the Jeesaki and some member of the committee, Beaulieu now cautioned them to let no man approach the shelter until he returned. Soon he was back. In his hands was the rope, all knots still tied! Beaulieu had lost the bet.

William Warren, the Ojibwe author we have previously quoted, was a self-ordained Christian missionary. He told in his "History of the Ojibways" something about his efforts to convert his people to Christianity. He was surprised that the elders of the tribes often knew the Old Testament stories of the Bible – but identified the heroes with Indian names. This led him to speculate that the Indian people could have been descendants of the "Ten Lost Tribes of Israel!"[9]

Differences Between Traditional Indian Culture and White Culture
Although cultures differ among the various tribes (there are at least eighteen families of languages in North America) the Ojibwe and the Sioux are very similar in the following characteristics as compared to white culture:

property
Indians tend to think in terms of communal ownership while whites stress ownership by the individual.

time
Indians think more in terms of the changing seasons; or monthly moons; whites are "clock watchers." Indians say that meetings will start "when we all get there;" whites say "the meeting will start at 1:00 sharp and be on time."

formality
Indians tend to be more informal; whites are more formal and systematic.

cooperation vs. competition
Indians stress cooperation; whites are more competitive. Even in games, Indians traditionally played more for fun of the activity while whites may be more concerned about winning.

family
Indians think in terms of the extended family, which includes aunts, uncles and cousins. Whites tend to focus more on the immediate family.

elders
Indians have a high respect for their elders and individuals tend to become more influential and more respected as they grow older. As whites retire or grow old they tend to have less influence.

nature
Indians think of themselves as close to or even as a part of nature. Whites may tend to be more interested in technology and other creations by humans and consider nature to be a gift of God for their personal enjoyment.

materialism
Indians teach their children to share with others and the accumulation of this world's goods isn't very important. Whites are more possessive and consider the accumulation of wealth as one way of elevating their status in the eyes of others.

history
Indians have long relied on oral history, passed down from generation to generation; whites tend to distrust oral history and are more inclined to believe the printed word.

assertiveness
Indians tend to be more passive; whites more aggressive.

eye contact
Indians consider it disrespectful to look someone in the eye; whites believe eye contact improves communication.

An Indian View of Leadership

Leaders should be
- charismatic,
- skilled at something,
- persuasive and
- spiritual in nature.

As we conclude this chapter with its descriptions of the cultures of the Dakota Sioux and the Ojibwe, we might speculate where their villages were located on Gull Lake. First, we must remember that the lake was inhabited off and on for at least 4,000 years and it is therefore likely that there were village sites at some time on all or nearly all pieces of high and dry ground whether on points, bays or islands. However, since the lake level has been raised nearly six feet by the dam on the Gull River, we can assume that most of the early sites are now under water. We do know from the journals and records of explorers, traders and missionaries that there were villages on:

- Mission Point on the south end of Gull Lake (Madden's)
- Gull Point (formerly Squaw Point), including both sides of the point and both sides of the dam site south and east of the base of the point,
- the narrows between Gull and Round Lakes, including the area between Round and Long Lakes and the east shore of Gull Lake between the narrows and the St. Columba Mission site – which is also called Mission point,
- Dutchman's Bluff, both on and below the bluff, and
- Sandy Point and just north of the point..

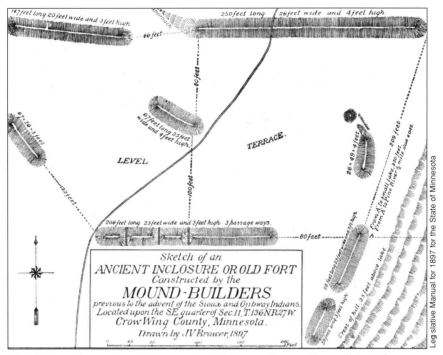

Fort Flatmouth was given that name by J.V. Brower because it was that Ojibwe chief who described its location near Pine River to William Warren, author of "History of the Ojibways." We really don't know if it was an Indian fort or just the remains of a village.

Drawing on Elden Johnson's report to the Corps of Engineers in 1979 entitled, "Cultural Resources Investigation of the Reservoir Shorelines of Gull Lake, Leech Lake, Pine River and Lake Pokegema" and reports of local land owners, the following sites on the shores of Gull Lake provided a significant number of artifacts to indicate possible village sites in addition to the five listed on the previous page:

- North end of Upper Gull east of the bridge over Spring Creek,
- Northeast end of Steamboat Bay,
- North end of the lake – southwest of Schaefer's Point,
- North peninsula at the channel between Gull and Bass Lake and
- South of the narrows of Upper Gull; east side between Gull and Lost Lakes.

The mound sites listed on pages 12 & 13 are also likely village sites.

Johnson listed several other sites where just a few artifacts were found. These may or may not have been village sites. It is interesting (but not surprising) that many sites produced artifacts of more than one culture.

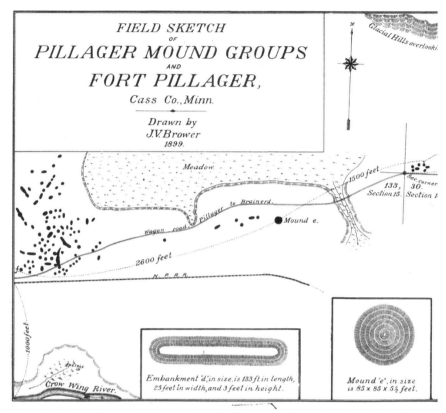

Drawing by J.V. Brower in his report to the Minnesota Historical Society in 1899.

J.V. Brower, in his report to the Minnesota Historical Society (1899) entitled "Memoirs of Explorations in the Basin of the Mississippi" talked about the remains of fortified Indian villages found across the woodlands of what is now Minnesota, including the Gull Lake area. He identified one such location as being one mile upstream from Motley on the west bank of the Crow Wing River and another on Red Sand Lake. He named the latter "Fort Pillager" because of its nearness to the community of that name. He believed the elongated mounds found at both sites were the remains of village fortifications. Subsequent historians and archeologists have expressed their doubts about his fortification theory and suggest they are the remains of permanent dwellings of the Blackduck Indians or their predecessors — or possibly the Dakota Sioux. The latter had earthen dwellings on Mille Lacs Lake at the time they were driven from that area by the Ojibwe. Since human remains have not been found in these long, narrow mounds, they remain somewhat of a mystery.

As we have said, there were probably no more than four major villages

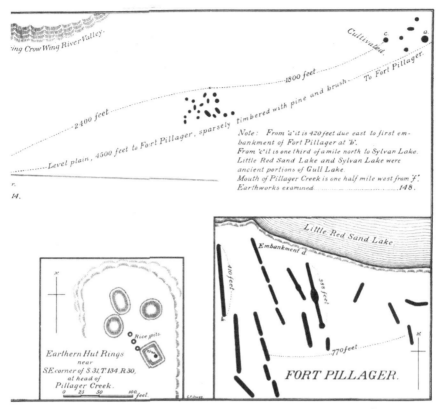

Brower called the mounds group in the lower right-hand corner "Fort Pillager" because it was fairly close to that community.

on Gull lake during the Ojibwe occupation. Each major village had its own chief and governance. Sometimes there was a war chief in addition to the civil chief. Since all of the villages on the lake at any one time were all Sioux or all Ojibwe, one would assume they got along well and there were no major conflicts. There was at least one exception, however: Chief Hole-in-the-Day II and Chief Bad Boy did have a serious rivalry. Bad Boy was unhappy with the U.S. Government's designation of Hole-in-the-Day as "principal chief" of the Gull-Crow Wing region and the latter was unhappy with Bad Boy because he had captured three Indians (probably Hole-in-the-Day's men) who had killed a white itinerant peddler. Bad Boy turned them over to white authorities to the south. A white citizen's posse overtook the sheriff and his captives at Swan River and killed the Indians. Hole-in-the-Day swore he would kill Bad Boy. At this point Bad Boy and his villagers moved to Mille Lacs Lake.

It should be noted that "principal chiefs" were quite powerful. They negotiated and signed the treaties with the U.S. Government. They were usually recognized as such on the recommendations of missionaries and traders in the area and because local Indians held them in high esteem. The government probably had second thoughts about Hole-in-the-Day II after he burned the St. Columba Mission and threatened to kill all the whites in the area!

In summary, the Dakota Sioux took control of Gull Lake in the 1600's and remained in undisputed control until 1739. From 1739 to 1766, Gull Lake was a part of Minnesota's "no man's land". It was a time when it was impossible to establish permanent villages. Both Dakota Sioux and Ojibwe war parties roamed the woodlands. Few white traders entered the woodlands during those years. Not only was there an element of danger, but with all the fighting there was little time to trap, so few furs were available.

It was in 1766 that an army of Ojibwe invaded the woodlands from the east and soundly defeated the Dakotas. From that time on, permanent villages were established by the Ojibwe on the woodland lakes. Although there may have been temporary Ojibwe villages on Gull Lake before 1800, we know that was the year Chief Curly Head established the first permanent Ojibwe village.

Thus, when the early explorers, traders and missionaries reached the lake after 1800, they found the Ojibwe firmly in control.

Footnotes

[1]Those living in the area we now call Minnesota are usually referred to as Dakotas; those living in what are now North and South Dakota as the Nakota and Lakota. The Nakota are identified with the Sisseton Band.

[2]The tribe was originally referred to as "Chippewa". In later years, "Ojibwe" became more popular. Today, many use "Anishinaubay."

[3]LaPointe was occupied by the Hurons and the Ottawas for about twenty years prior to the take over by the Ojibwe.

[4]Although it was the Sioux from the prairies of what is now North Dakota (either Lakota or Nakota) who attacked the French, it was the Dakota Sioux of what is now Minnesota who were the targets of revenge.

[5]Named for George Catlin, an artist and explorer who claimed to be the discoverer of the pipestone quarries. Others were actually there before him but he originally received the credit.

[6]Periods of mourning were often characterized by much crying and loud wailing.

[7]The real John Tanner was kidnapped from his missionary parents in Ohio and raised in the Minnesota-Ontario boundary waters area by Ottawa Indians. As an adult, he was an important leader of his adopted people. He was associated with men like Lord Selkirk (head of the Hudson's Bay Co.) and Henry Schoolcraft (Discoverer of the source of the Mississippi River).

[8]John's Indian name.

[9]A theory also held by the Mormon faith.

CHAPTER III

Gull Lake's Role in the 100 Year Dakota – Ojibwe War

In the last chapter we saw how the Sioux – Ojibwe contest for control of the northern Minnesota woodlands began in the 1730s. The great victories of the Ojibwe and their allies in 1766 did not end the conflict; it continued with few interruptions up to the time of the Civil War.

If we consider this in the perspective of the history of the United States, the conflict began 40 years before the start of the Revolutionary War and ended during the Civil War! Four generations of fighting. In 1862, following the white-Sioux conflict in the Mankato-New Ulm area, the military drove the Sioux out of the state into the Dakotas and Canada, thus ending the potential for fighting between the Ojibwe and the Sioux. During the more than 100 years of fighting, the Ojibwe war parties were made-up of warriors from all of the major lakes of the northern Minnesota woodlands—from the Canadian border down to Mille Lacs Lake. Although the Cree were ahead of the Ojibwe in establishing villages on the northern most lakes after the Sioux fled, they moved back north into Canada after a relative short stay.

The following are some of the major battles which took place in the Gull Lake-Crow Wing area or in which Gull Lake villages participated during the more than 100 years of conflict:

The Battle at the Mouth of the Crow Wing

It was 1768. The Dakota Sioux had been driven from their strongholds in northern Minnesota but had not given up. They had even been forced from their Mille Lacs Lake headquarters village when the Ojibwe blew up their earthen houses by dropping gunpowder down the smoke holes. It was from their new headquarters village at the mouth of the Rum River that a small army of about 200 Sioux braves launched a raid against the new Ojibwe capital on Sandy Lake.

At the same time, an Ojibwe war party of about seventy men moved south down the Mississippi with the Rum River village as their objective. The Dakotas proceeded up the Mississippi (but chose to take the Crow Wing cutoff), then traveled up the Gull River, across Gull, Long and Whitefish Lakes, then up to Pine River and across a series of lakes leading to Boy River and Leech Lake – on the way to Sandy Lake (because there was less current to fight). Thus the two war parties did not meet on their way to their respective objectives.

Apparently the Ojibwe did not find any indication that the Dakota Sioux had traveled north only days before. They were evidently totally surprised to find the Rum River village deserted, with the women and children safely protected elsewhere. Surprise turned to horror when the Ojibwe realized the possible significance of the empty village. Their worst fears were to be realized. The Dakotas had fallen on a helpless Sandy Lake village and slaughtered everyone except thirty young women whom they took captive along with an older woman to care for them. The Ojibwe wasted no time looking for the hidden Dakota Sioux women and children but hurried back up river–intent on finding a battlefield of their liking to ambush the Sioux. They reached the mouth of the Crow Wing without encountering the enemy, and here they finally discovered camp signs left by the Dakotas on their way north. They dared to go no further because they were not sure which river the Sioux would come–the Crow Wing or the Mississippi. They quickly dug in on a bluff on the east bank of the Mississippi overlooking both rivers (where their excavations may be seen to this day as a part of Crow Wing State Park). They did not have long to wait. A scout reported that the Dakota Sioux war party was on its way down the Mississippi. They stopped across from Crow Wing Island, where they forced their captives to serve them breakfast, in full view of their loved ones who were anxiously lying in ambush.

As the story goes, the old woman whose life had been spared to care for the captives turned out to be a real heroine. She had quietly reminded her charges that there was a good chance they would meet the returning men from their village somewhere along the river. If and when this should happen, she urged the women to overturn the canoes and swim towards the rifle fire. And that is exactly what happened. The unsuspecting Dakotas were caught completely off guard and suffered heavy casualties. The Ojibwe had chosen their battleground well. Here the Mississippi narrowed and made a sharp turn, the faster current bringing the Dakota Sioux into close range, but they were not about to give up their captives or leave without a good fight. Incensed over the sudden turn of events and the fact they had been outsmarted by their captives–women at that (Indian warriors of that time were real male chauvinists!)–they placed the

Ojibwe under siege. When frontal attacks proved too costly, they crossed the river and circled behind them on land, but the Ojibwe were too well protected and continued to get the better of the battle. At last, the Dakotas decided "discretion was indeed the better part of valor" and reluctantly turned their canoes downstream.

A Truce

The only significant truce during the 100 Years War took place around the 1770s when the Ojibwe and the Dakota Sioux agreed to hunt and trap in peace during the winter months in the area around the Long Prairie and the Crow Wing Rivers.

These hunting grounds were so important to both the Sioux and the Ojibwe that when neither was able to conclusively drive the other from it, a winter truce was negotiated several years running. Prior to this time, a hunter might very well return to his camp at night with a scalp or two hanging from his belt as well as furs taken during the day. The truce also made it possible to take the entire family on the winter hunt.

So good was the hunting that the Ojibwe came from as far away as Leech Lake and Sandy Lake as well as Gull Lake. These villages retained a close relationship over the years and it was their custom to rendezvous at Gull Lake or the mouth of the Crow Wing on their way to the winter hunting grounds. The Mille Lacs Ojibwe also wintered in the Crow Wing-Long Prairie areas.

The virgin pine forests of the north were not good habitat for wildlife because insufficient light could filter through to nourish the undergrowth which provides food for both birds and animals. Because of the scarcity of game in the Winter and the thick ice covering the lakes, it made sense to move to the edge of the prairies where food and furs were more readily available. The Sioux came from as far away as the prairies of present day North and South Dakota and included the Wahpetons and Sissetons as well as other Dakota bands. They were probably drawn by the beaver.

The Ojibwe bands from Leech, Sandy, Gull and other lakes then traveled up the Long Prairie and Crow Wing Rivers. They were especially attracted by the herds of elk and buffalo that grazed in the area, as well as the beaver in the streams. The Dakotas were usually there first and already settled in their hide-covered teepees. After warring back and forth all summer, the only way the Ojibwe could be certain the winter truce would again be in effect was to directly approach the Sioux village and offer to smoke the pipe of peace. Dressed for the occasion and well-armed, a vanguard—not so large as to be threatening but not so small as to be easy prey—would march right into the Sioux village. The bearer of the peace pipe and the banner carriers led the procession. The customary response of the Dakotas was to welcome the Ojibwe with a volley of rifle fire. Sometimes the singing bullets were so near the ears of the visitors that it seemed the "name of the game" was to come as close as possible without scoring! Once it was clear that a truce was desired, the Ojibwe were welcomed into the lodges of the Sioux where they smoked the peace pipe and feasted on the best available food—sometimes literally beneath the scalps of their fellow tribesmen which may have been taken as recently as the past summer and now hung suspended from the lodge poles. The Ojibwe had a word for this ceremony; they called it "Pin-ding-u-daud-e-win," which is translated, "to enter into one another's lodges."

An interesting custom during these periods of truce was for warriors to adopt "brothers" from among the traditional enemies of the other tribes. Often they were considered as replacements for special friends or brothers lost in battle. There are many tales of adopted brothers being spared during subsequent raids or battles. It is told that the relationship between the two tribes sometimes became so friendly that there was intermarrying and even the exchanging of wives.

The End of the Truce — Chief Yellow Hair's Revenge

Chief Flat Mouth of Leech Lake was the most able and significant leader of the Ojibwe in the 1800s. We will speak much more of him shortly. His father, Wa-son-aun-e-qua or "Yellow Hair" however, was somewhat of a scoundrel. According to Flat Mouth, Chief Yellow Hair did not inherit his title, but achieved his leadership role through a remarkable knowledge of medicines, including poisons. It is said that his enemies lost their lives in a mysterious and unaccountable manner. His own son called him "vindictive" and "revengeful" and said that he retaliated against his enemies two-fold. It is likely that Yellow Hair was a follower of a well known false prophet or "Shaman" of that day. This medicine man turned witch doctor garnered a tremendous following among the Ojibwe and persuaded them to forsake their traditional Midewiwin religion. He claimed to have a new revelation from the Great Spirit and urged all to throw away their little medicine bags and follow him. A religious rally of sorts was held at the location of present day Detroit. However, when it was discovered he could not raise the dead some of his followers had brought to him and when he was found hiding in a hollow tree when he was supposed to be in heaven conferring with the Great Spirit, his disciples (including Flat Mouth) deserted him.

Typical of Yellow Hair's vengeful spirit is the story of how the Winter truce between the Sioux and the Ojibwe was broken:

As we have mentioned, the Ojibwe and Dakota Sioux had entered into a truce so that they could hunt and trap in peace during the winter in the

Crow Wing – Long Prairie Rivers area. We have also stated that to cement the truce, it had become the custom of individual warriors to adopt one another from different tribes as brothers. Yellow Hair and a Dakota Sioux warrior adopted each other and became friends. Yellow Hair, who already spoke some Sioux, perfected his mastery of the tongue. In the spring, just before their return to Leech Lake, four Ojibwe children, including Yellow Hair's eldest son, (Flat Mouth's brother) were murdered while at play by a marauding band of Sioux from the west.

Yellow Hair urged revenge. His followers and other Ojibwe chiefs felt this would be useless because the war party was long gone. Yellow Hair, however, argued for revenge against any available Sioux, including those with whom they had a peace treaty. Others urged moderation, and the chief finally agreed to return to Leech Lake with the bodies of the children. After burial, however, Yellow Hair and five of his warriors headed back for the Long Prairie River, intent upon revenge. They encountered the Sandy Lake band who were on their way home. The leadership of this group perceived Yellow Hair's purpose and tried to dissuade him, knowing that a resumption of hostilities would escalate making it impossible to hunt and trap in peace during future winters. They even gave him more than enough gifts to "cover" the death of his son. Yellow Hair accepted the gifts and pretended to return to Leech Lake. However, when they were out of sight, he again turned southwest.

William Warren in his *"History of the Ojibways"* described the eventual gratification of Yellow Hair's loss thus:

On the head waters of Crow River, nearly two hundred miles from the point of his departure, Yellow Hair at last caught up with the two lodges of his enemies. At the first peep of dawn in the morning, the Dakotas were startled from their quiet slumbers by the fear-striking Ojibwe war-whoop, and as the men arose to grasp their arms and the women and children jumped up in affright, the bullets of the enemy fell amongst them, causing wounds and death. After the first moments of surprise, the men of the Dakotas returned the fire of the enemy, and for many minutes the fight raged hotly. An interval in the incessant firing at last took place, and the voice of a Dakota, apparently wounded, called out to the Ojibways, "Alas! why is it that I die? I thought my road was clear before and behind me, and that the skies were cloudless above me. My mind dwelt only on good and blood was not in my thoughts."

Yellow Hair recognized the voice of the warrior who had agreed to be his adopted brother during the late peace between their respective tribes. He understood his words, but his wrong was great, and his heart had become as hard as flint. He answered: "My brother, I too thought that the skies were cloudless above me, and I lived without fear; but a wolf came and destroyed my young; he traced from the country of the Dakotas. My brother, for this you die!"

"My brother, I knew it not," answered the Dakota—" it was none of my people, but the wolves of the prairies."

The Ojibwe warrior now quietly filled and lit his pipe, and while he smoked, the silence was only broken by the groans of the wounded and the suppressed wail of bereaved mothers. Having finished his smoke, he laid aside his pipe and once more he called out to the Dakotas:

"My brother, have you still in your lodge a child who will take the place of my lost one, whom your wolves have devoured? I have come a great distance to behold once more my young as I once beheld him, and I return not on my tracks till I am satisfied!"

The Dakotas, thinking that he wished for a captive to adopt instead of his deceased child, and happy to escape certain destruction at such a cheap sacrifice, took one of the surviving children, a little girl, and decking it with such finery and ornaments as they possessed, they sent her out to the covet of the Ojibwe warrior. The innocent little girl came forward, but no sooner was she within reach of the avenger, than he grasped her by the hair of the head and loudly exclaiming—"I sent for thee that I might do with you as your people did to my child. I wish to behold thee as I once beheld him," he deliberately scalped her alive, and sent her shrieking back to her agonized parents.

After this cold-blooded act, the fight was renewed with great fury. Yellow Hair rushed desperately forward, and by main force he pulled down one of the Dakota lodges. As he did so the wounded warrior, his former adopted brother, discharged his gun at his breast, which the active and wary Ojibwe adroitly dodged, the contents killed one of his comrades who had followed him close at his back. Not a being in that Dakota lodge survived; the other, being bravely defended, was left standing; and Yellow Hair, with his four surviving companions, returned homeward, their vengeance fully glutted, and having committed a deed which ever after became the topic of the lodge circles of their people.

Fortunately, Flat Mouth differed in may ways from his father. The practice of using poisons, for example, was abandoned once he succeeded him as chief.

Dakotas Attack A French Trading Post
At The Mouth Of The Partridge River

One winter in the early 1780's, shortly after the truce had been broken, the Ojibwe of the northern lakes made their usual migration to the Crow Wing and Long Prairie Rivers. That year a French trader had constructed a trading post where the Partridge River enters the Crow Wing.

The Ojibwe called the trader "Ah-wish-to-yah," which meant "Blacksmith." Several voyageurs were there with him at the time and together with the Pillager-Ojibwe hunters and trappers totaled about forty men working out of the post. Most of the Indians had brought their families with them, even though they knew there was a good chance of an encounter with Dakota Sioux hunters or even war parties. The trader was also aware of the danger, but a heavy population of beaver had drawn him there.

Expecting the worst, the men erected a log barricade around the post and the wigwams.

Late one night, ten of the Ojibwe hunters awakened those at the post with the alarming news that a sizable band of Dakotas were in the area. They had crossed their trail and identified them by the lingering smell of tobacco (which was distinctly different from the ground inner-bark of the kinnikinnick smoked by the Ojibwe). The Dakota Sioux were following a trail which would lead them to a small, defenseless camp of hunters. Craftily, the Ojibwe circled ahead of the Dakotas and crossed the trail, hoping to lure them to the more easily defended barricade at the trading post. The strategy worked. By the time the Dakota Sioux arrived, the barricade had been strengthened and nearly twenty men (French and Ojibwe) were ready for the attack.

The party of Dakota Sioux was large indeed – about two hundred braves – but whereas the men at the post were all armed with guns, the Dakota Sioux were forced to depend on bows and arrows and had only a half-dozen rifles among them.

The huge war party finally appeared on the bank across from the trading post. Confident in their numerical superiority, they leisurely put on their paint, feathers and other ornaments. Then, sounding their war whoops, they charged across the ice sending out a cloud of arrows into the fortification. But the defenders were well-protected and their rifle fire was devastating. No Dakota Sioux reached the barricade. With a change in strategy, the Dakotas began firing their arrows almost straight up, lobbing them – like mortar fire – into the compound. The shower of barbed missiles was more effective and two Ojibwe hunters were wounded seriously enough to take them out of action. Some took refuge in the post itself. But in the end, the rifles proved to be more than an equalizing factor and a frustrated Dakota Sioux war party – with a greatly diminished supply of arrows – finally recognized the futility of the situation.

Before leaving, they cut holes in the river ice and gave their dead a watery burial.[1]

Shortly after their departure, other hunters and trappers who had heard the shooting arrived at the post – about twenty reinforcements in all. Realizing that the Dakotas were nearly out of arrows, they wanted to press their advantage by pursuing them. The trader argued to the contrary and finally prevailed.

It is interesting that at this date, about 1780, the Dakotas had so few guns. It may have been that they came from the prairies farther west and had, therefore, little opportunity to procure them. If so, then they were probably Nakotas or Lakotas and not Dakotas.

How the Gull, Cass, Leech and Other Central Lakes Ojibwe came to be called "Pillagers"

This was not a battle between the Ojibwe and the Sioux, but it was a significant incident in our area history. It took place at the mouth of Pillager Creek, where it enters the Crow Wing.

Because of the inter-tribal wars, few traders had ventured into the woodlands area for many years. In the spring of 1781, a trader, accompanied by a handful of voyageurs, traveled up the Mississippi. He chose the Crow Wing cut-off and camped at the mouth of what is now called Pillager Creek. Here he took ill and was forced to rest. A band of Leech Lake Ojibwe–perhaps out to make sure there were no Sioux war parties in the area–had traveled down the Gull Lake-Gull River route and came across the sick trader and his men. They were most anxious to do business. The trader, unfortunately, was too ill to negotiate. The young braves, however, were not to be denied.

As the story goes, they at first intended to leave items of equal value to those taken, but when a cask of "firewater" was discovered and consumed, their judgment was clouded. As matters grew worse, the voyageurs placed the trader in his canoe and headed back down the river. The next day, near the present site of Sauk Rapids, the trader died.

It is said that the Ojibwe bands from Gull Lake to Leech Lake received the name "Pillagers" because of the pillaging that took place here. Even other Indians called them "Muk-im-dua-Wine-Wug", which means to take by force. The city, the creek and the tribe all received their names from this incident.

Treaties between the U.S. Government and Native American Tribes use the word "Pillager" to identify the Ojibwe of this area from the Crow Wing River to Leech Lake.

The Plague

During the 100 Years War, an enemy far more sinister than warriors from rival tribes hit the villages of what is now Minnesota. We know it as smallpox.

The disease had been in Europe for centuries and many of the whites who came to this continent had survived the illness or built up an immunity. The Native Americans, however, were extremely vulnerable. In 1782 it spread like wildfire from village to village. At this time Gull Lake was a part of the "no man's land" so there may have been no villages as such on the lake when the plague struck. There are two explanations of how it reached the area we now know as Minnesota:

Following the taking of the trader's goods at Pillager Creek, Ojibwe leaders decided to send a delegation to Mackinac–then a British fort–to make amends for harassing the trader and his voyageurs. There had been only a few whites in the area during the first part of the 100 years War and the Ojibwe leadership feared the confrontation would discourage traders from entering the area. The delegation was well received at Mackinac and were even given trade goods by the British. On their return, they stopped at Fond du Lac to display these items to other Ojibwe. Almost overnight the travelers, as well as members of that village, took sick with smallpox. In a matter of days, Fond du Lac was all but wiped out and several members of the delegation also died, including their leader. On the survivors return to Leech Lake, the disease was spread to other villages. It was thought the source of the infestation was the whites at Mackinac and that the germs were transmitted on the trade goods. It is also believed that smallpox entered Minnesota from the west. The carriers in this case were a party of Assiniboines, Cree, and Ojibwe who had come upon a village in North Dakota–either Mandans or Gros Ventres–which was experiencing a smallpox devastation. There was little resistance, and the war party took many scalps. When they returned to the boundary waters with their infected trophies they spread the disease across what is now northern Minnesota and into Ontario. Some historians believe this may have been the source of infection in Fond du Lac and that it arrived simultaneously with the Leech Lake Indians returning from Mackinac.

Whatever the source, the devastation was beyond present-day comprehension. The huge village at Sandy Lake was reduced to seven wigwams. Other villages were even less fortunate; sometimes there were no survivors. Jean Baptiste Cadotte, the French trader, sent this only slightly exaggerated message to Mackinac: "All the Indians from Fond du Lac, Rainy Lake, Sandy Lake and surrounding places are dead from smallpox."

But all did not die, and the villages were eventually repopulated.

Gull Lake Ojibwe Leaders Make Their Impact on the 100 Years War

Curly Head (Ba-be-sig-undi-bay)

The first Ojibwe leader to make his mark on Gull Lake was the legendary Curly Head. He was the principal chief of the Gull Lake and Crow Wing bands and provided the leadership that made it possible to hold this area against repeated advances by the Dakota Sioux from the time of his arrival on the lake in 1800 until his death twenty-five years later (1825). We have no photographs or eye witness accounts of why this chief had such an unusual name, but it is likely that his hair was indeed curly and this would set him apart from other Indians. (Who knows, he may have had some Viking blood?)

As stated earlier, the Ojibwe, in 1766. were finally successful in driving the Dakota Sioux from the woodlands of what is now Minnesota. Following that date, attempts were made to establish villages in the conquered territory. This was done with great difficulty because Sioux raiding parties returned north again and again and would sometimes annihilate entire villages. Men, women and children were all killed. Sometimes, however, young women were taken as slaves.

As more and more Ojibwe migrated into the area from both south and north of Lake Superior, the settlements finally became more secure. Curly Head was among the Ojibwe who first settled on Sandy Lake. We don't know exactly when he arrived or how or when he received the rank of chief. We do know he was a part of the leadership on Sandy Lake in 1800 when it was decided that permanent villages needed to be established farther south to secure the entire woodlands area against Dakota Sioux war parties. This would also help insure the safety of the more northern villages. Since Gull Lake was a strategic location on the alternate (to the Mississippi) canoe route north, it was chosen as the site of one of these permanent settlements. Curly Head and his band either volunteered or were chosen to move there.

The northeast corner of Gull Lake was selected as the village site, perhaps because what we now call Dutchman's Bluff provided a perfect view of most of the lake. Any effort by the Dakotas to use this route would be totally visible. The bluff may have been a Sioux village and a Blackduck site before that. Curly Head remained here until his death in 1825 and was successful in preventing the Dakota Sioux from using this north-south canoe route. Later, villages would be established by sub-chiefs on both Mission Points, Gull (formerly Squaw) Point, Sand Point and the parcel of ground between Gull, Round and Long Lakes. Curly Head was recognized by both the Indians and the whites as the principal chief of an area described sometimes as "the Gull Lake–Mississippi band" and other times as the "Gull Lake–Crow Wing band". He was surely a gifted leader and was characterized to the author, William Warren, thus: "He was a father to his people. They looked on him as children do a parent; and his slightest wish was immediately performed. His lodge was always full of meat, to which the hungry and destitute were ever welcome. The traders vied with one another who should treat him best, and the presents which he received at their hands he always distributed to his people without reserve. When he had plenty, his people wanted not."

Curly Head was a contemporary and ally of Flat Mouth the Elder, the great Leech Lake chieftain. The two joined forces on at least one occasion to wage war against the Dakotas. A raiding party was organized to avenge the deaths of Flat Mouth's nephew and two of Curly Head's allies—Waub-o-jeeg II and She-shebe. The latter two and their families were killed and scalped while fishing through the ice on Mille Lacs Lake. She-shebe is remembered for his heroic efforts at Battle Point on Cross Lake, where a camp of Ojibwe returning from their winter hunt were ambushed and nearly annihilated (1800). The Sioux war party reportedly consisted of nearly 400 braves while the Ojibwe, according to their report, had only half that number, including women and children. Waub-o-jeeg was a war chief for Curly Head.

Flat Mouth's nephew was killed by the Dakotas after the Mille Lacs Lake incident, and it was his death that motivated Flat Mouth to join forces with Curly Head in teaching the Sioux a lesson.

A large war party from Leech Lake joined a Gull Lake contingent on the Crow Wing. There were probably about 200 warriors in all. They traveled up the Long Prairie River, which enters the Crow Wing just south of present day Motley, until they reached a Dakota Sioux village of about 40 lodges. The Ojibwe were undetected and surrounded the village under cover of darkness. They attacked at dawn with the advantage of complete surprise. The Dakotas fought bravely but suffered heavy casualties in the initial attack and were under-manned to start with. The battle raged all day; in the end, only seven Sioux survived. Flat Mouth and Curly Head were satisfied that the deaths of their relative and friends had been avenged and the seven were allowed to live—reportedly out of respect for their bravery. The Ojibwe left with the coming of darkness, but not before killing all of the Dakotas' horses. The animals were of little value in the woodlands where water transportation was more efficient.

This incident is an example of how Native American Tribes weren't very selective in taking revenge. If the culprits weren't available, revenge was taken on other villages of that tribe.

Firm Ground (Song-a-cumig) and Hole-in-the-Day I (Pugona-geshig)

In Curly Head's last years he was served by two protégés—brothers—whom he named as his "pipe bearers:" the older of the brothers (by two or three years) was Song-a-cumig or "Firm Ground," and the other was to become the famous Pogona-geshig or Hole-in-the-Day I. The brothers had come to this part of Minnesota with the Cass Expedition of 1820, for which they were awarded medals by that famous governor of the Michigan Territory.

It is worth noting that Lewis Cass served 18 years as governor of the Michigan Territory (which for awhile included Minnesota) and then went on to be Secretary of War (1831-36), Ambassador to France (1836-42), U.S. Senator from the new state of Michigan, Secretary of State under President Buchanan and then three times sought the Democratic nomination for president. On the third try he was successful in winning the endorsement but lost to Zachary Taylor. In Minnesota, Cass Lake and Cass County are named for him.

It was Governor Cass who brought the famous brothers, Song-a-cumig or Firm Ground and Pugona-geshig or Hole-in-the-Day I to central Minnesota and eventually the brothers arrived at Gull Lake. It should be noted that Henry Schoolcraft, who discovered the source of the Mississippi on a later trip, was also a member of the Cass party.

Hole-in-the-Day joined the expedition at Mackinac. It is amazing how well-traveled Indians were in that day. The young brave was visiting traders there and became enthralled with the idea of joining Cass as he journeyed first to the Ojibwe country of

Lewis B. Cass (1782-1866). Governor of Michigan Territory and Democratic candidate for president.

what is now Minnesota and then down the Mississippi into Sioux territory. The purposes of the expedition was to learn more about the huge Michigan Territory and to make sure everyone therein knew it was part of the United States. Hole-in-the-Day persuaded the local traders to recommend him to Cass and he was accepted. It is possible that Firm Ground was there, but he may have joined the party later when it reached Lake Superior where the brothers home village was located. We know he was with the Cass expedition when it was in what is now Minnesota.

When the expedition reached Sault Ste. Marie, Hole-in-the-Day proved to be a great asset to Governor Cass. The Indians there were loyal to the British and threatened to massacre the Cass party which had only 65 members. Following a speech by the governor, Hole-in-the-Day fired a borrowed rifle to get attention and then gave a rousing speech to the Indians in their own Ojibwe tongue—urging them to support the Americans. When he asked, "are any of you with me?" a large number (possibly over 100) came to stand with him, but the vast majority did not commit themselves. A long and worrisome twenty-four hours followed, but in the end, the Indians were won over and cooperated with the Americans. Hole-in-the-Day was an instant hero and Governor Cass responded thus:

"Through the authority invested in me, Sir, by our Great White Father in Washington, I hereby designate you a Chief, now and forever after in the eyes of every American. With you we shall hereafter deal directly, as the Chief of your own band of these faithful and dedicated warriors, and of all others of any band who may subsequently choose to join you!"

Cass then presented Hole-in-the-Day with a medal and an American flag and told him that he could keep the rifle.

We know that Firm Ground at some point was also presented with a medal by the governor.

It is not clear how the brothers came to the attention of Curly Head, but he must have been impressed because he made them his pipe bearers—a special honor often leading to becoming a chief. Although Cass had already named Hole-in-the-Day a chief and the young warrior had become the leader of the Ojibwe traveling with the expedition, that wasn't as prestigious as being a pipe bearer to Curly Head, who was recognized as the principal chief of the Gull Lake–Mississippi–Crow Wing region.

Early in the 1820's, Hole-in-the-Day became a sub-chief at Sandy Lake.

In 1825, Curly Head traveled to Prairie du Chien (Wisconsin) where a peace treaty was signed between the Ojibwe and the Sioux. It should be noted that the treaty proved to be worthless. On his way home, Curly Head took ill and died. Some contagious disease was evidently present at the peace conference, because many Indians, both Ojibwe and Sioux, never made it back to their villages. At this point, or possibly earlier, Hole-in-the-Day moved back to Gull Lake where he became Curly Head's successor as principal chief.

Firm Ground, although two or three year older then Hole-in-the-Day, never achieved the status of his younger brother. He was recognized as a war chief, however, and did head his own village on Pine River for a time. He achieved fame at an early age (ten) when he tagged along with Chiefs Curly Head and Flat Mouth when they attacked the Sioux village on the Long Prairie River (as described earlier).[4] Somehow he scalped a dying Dakota warrior!

Firm Ground and Hole-in-the-Day remained close and worked as a team — occasionally joined by a younger brother whose name was Zhegud or "the Branch". The latter spent most of his time, however, in the village on Lake Superior where all three had grown-up. Together, they and their followers thwarted every attempt by the Dakota Sioux to send a war party north. When Firm Ground died before the age of 50, he was eligible to wear 38 feathers in his headdress, each symbolizing the death of a Sioux Indian.

We know Curly Head and the two Hole-in-the-Days were headquartered at the northeastern end of Gull Lake and that as principal chiefs they ruled the entire Gull Lake–Crow Wing–Mississippi region (as far east as present day Riverton) from 1800 until 1868 when Hole-in-the-Day the Younger died and nearly all of the Gull Lake Ojibwe had been moved to White Earth, but we know little about the sub-chiefs who governed other villages on the lake. We do know, however, that Waub-o-Jeeg III, a contemporary of both Hole-in-the-Days, headed the village at the base of Gull Point and that at the same time, Ma-cou-da (or Bear's Heart) was a sub-chief at the north end of the lake. We are not sure just where.

Waub-o-Jeeg II was a war chief for Curly Head. His father, the original Waub-o-Jeeg, played a major role in driving the Fox and the Sac tribes out of northern Wisconsin. Although Algonquin related, these tribes were enemies of the Ojibwe.

John Johnson, the Ottawa Indian who was the principal deacon at St. Columba Mission, spoke of Chiefs Turtle and White Cloud as being part of the exodus to White Earth but we know nothing more about them. Chief Bad Boy's village was on and around the Mission Point on the northeast end of the lake. He provided the land on which the St. Columba Mission was built in 1852. There was also a sub-chief named Menomini who ruled on Sandy Point in the 1860's.

Courtesy Cass County Historical Society

Waub-o-jeeg II (White Fisher)

Carl Zapffe in his book, "The man Who Lived in Three Centuries," gives an interesting account of collaboration between the hero of his work, John Smith, and Chief Hole-in-the-Day I. It seems Hole-in-the-Day's medicine man had a vision of a Sioux village which could be easily conquered and said that he could lead his chief to its location. Hole-in-the-Day asked John Smith if he cared to join him. Zapffe gives this account of Smith's response and the expedition that followed:

"Not forgetting my early pledge to spill the blood of those who had murdered my sister and brother," later recorded Smith, "I consented gladly; and, summoning all the warriors of my then great tribe, we start-

ed out upon the warpath." The combined assault was headed by Hole-in-the-Day, though guided by the Medicine Man. Three days passed in transit; and on the morning of the fourth the stage of the stealthy approach began.

Sure enough! Exactly in the position predicted by the Medicine Man, there stood a Dakota village, lying peaceably in a small valley. From one of the lodges issued a thin and lazy column of smoke. Otherwise there was no noise, neither any signs of life.

Creeping with exceeding precaution, the warriors came within gunshot, and the Chief gave the fatal signal. A simultaneous volley thundered down the little valley, lead balls pouring with well-considered spacing into every one of the teepees. The only answer was the dismal howl of a dog.

Because Smith's sole purpose in agreeing to accompany Hole-in-the-Day was to discover an opportunity for revenging the deaths in his family, he now boldly stepped forward to take the initiative in bringing this battle to its hoped-for climax. Furthermore, deep inside he felt extremely confident "that no enemy bullet could kill me, as I hold a charmed life."

Not waiting to reload his gun, and grabbing nothing but his battle-ax, Smith raced to the nearest lodge—the one having a slight issue of smoke. He bounded right through the doorway and with such fierce energy as calculated to take any opponent by surprise. But he found nothing except the dog. The exciting wisps of smoke were issuing from a few lazy embers, apparently remaining from a fire that had been abandoned hours before. Plunging his tomahawk into the body of the unfortunate dog, Smith dashed back outside and ordered his warriors to search the village. All dwellings proved to be empty.

Hole-in-the-Day was so intensely angered over this useless enterprise that he immediately killed "Big Medicine Man."

After spending several years at Gull Lake, Hole-in-the-Day moved south to the mouth of the Crow Wing and, later, to the mouth of the Little Elk River, just north of the site of present-day Little Falls. Here he protected the southern frontier of the Ojibwe. At times the pressures from the Sioux were too much and he would be forced to retreat to Whitefish or to Rabbit Lake.

More fighting between Hole-in-the-Day's Warriors and the Dakota Sioux

In 1838, Hole-in-the-Day played a major role in a series of bloody confrontations between the Dakotas and the Ojibwe. In April of that year, he and a party of nine braves stumbled onto a camp of Sioux on the Chippewa River (a tributary of the Minnesota); they were mostly women and children temporarily separated from a hunting party. Professing peace, they were warmly welcomed and dined on dog meat—one of the Indians' choice delicacies. That night, on signal, Hole-in-the-Day and his men fell on the Sioux and killed all but three.

On August 2, Sioux relatives of the massacre victims had an opportunity for revenge. They surprised Hole-in-the-Day and five companions near Fort Snelling; one of the Indians with whom Hole-in-the-Day had exchanged clothing—or ornaments—was killed and another wounded (both were Ottawas). When one of the Sioux ran in to collect what he believed to be the scalp of Hole-in-the-Day, White Fisher, who was in the Ojibwe party, shot him. The famous Indian Agent, Taliaferro, came on the scene at that point, and the Sioux fled. The Ojibwe were taken to the fort and the Ottawa Indian was buried there. Hole-in-the-Day was escorted across the river and had to find his way home on his own.

When they heard of the incident, the chiefs of the neighboring Sioux villages came to the fort, as well as the leadership of the Red Wing band of Lake Pepin—to which the young Sioux belonged who had killed the Ottawa.

At the insistence of the commander of the fort, Major Plympton, two young braves were turned over to him and placed in custody, but the chiefs pleaded for their lives. After being satisfied that the Sioux leadership would properly punish their young warriors, Major Plympton released them to their custody. The punishment administered by the ranking Sioux braves to the culprits was traditional; their blankets, leggings and breech cloths were cut into small pieces; their hair was cut short (signifying great humiliation); and they were heavily flogged. One Ojibwe was dead; one Sioux was dead; the score was even, and it seemed peace would be continued.

However, the following year, 1839, Hole-in-the-Day with five hundred Gull Lake people, another hundred from the Crow Wing area, one hundred fifty from Leech Lake, and another contingent from Mille Lacs Lake all arrived at the St. Peter's Agency (by Fort Snelling) under the mistaken notion that they could collect certain annuities due them. Twelve hundred Sioux arrived at the agency for the same purpose (but under a different treaty). The Ojibwe were told they would have to go to La Pointe to collect what they had coming, but they were given some food. Surprisingly enough, the historic enemies got along well and even danced and played games together. After a month, the food ran out and the Ojibwe began their return journeys to the north. Two of Hole-in-the-Day's men who were related to the warrior shot the previous year stopped at the fort to weep over the grave of their slain kinsman. Inspired to seek revenge, they approached the Lake Calhoun camp of the Dakotas at

The pictorial signatures of three powerful Minnesota Chiefs: Flat Mouth, Shakopee, and Hole-In-The-Day I.

night—some think with the knowledge and encouragement of Hole-in-the-Day. At daybreak they killed a departing hunter named Nika. The slain Sioux turned out to be a highly respected warrior, brother-in-law of the chief, and nephew of the famous medicine man, Red Bird.

Revenge came quickly. One contingent of about one hundred warriors—under Little Crow (a predecessor of the Little Crow who led the Sioux uprising in 1862)—surprised a large band of Ojibwe near the present site of Stillwater. They were finally driven off but not before killing twenty-one and wounding twenty-nine Ojibwe. The second contingent, under Red Bird, pursued the Mille Lacs Lake band. Before leaving, the pipe of war was passed down the rows of Sioux warriors and Red Bird followed, laying hands on the heads of each and swearing them to strike without pity, taking no captives. After locating the Mille Lacs Indians, they waited until most braves had gone on ahead to hunt. The old men, women and children left behind were at first easy prey, but the hunters returned quickly and a bitter struggle ensued. The Sioux took seventy scalps but lost seventeen braves of their own, including Red Bird and his son. The Ojibwe scalps were hung from their lodge poles at Lake Calhoun and the celebrating went on for a month.

Taliaferro was keenly disappointed and left the agency soon thereafter. He had taken a special interest and pride in the Lake Calhoun settlement where he had been quite successful in encouraging agricultural practices. He had given the settlement the name "Eatonville." And so the bloody conflict between the two great tribes continued for another generation.

Hole-in-the-Day I dies young

Chief Hole-in-the-Day I died in 1847 at an age of about forty-six years. he was returning from Pig's Eye (St. Paul) where he had become drunk and was being carried home on the floor of a wagon. As the entourage was crossing the Platte River he fell from the wagon and was critically injured. His warriors carried him to a nearby home; here he regained consciousness long enough to pass on the mantle of authority and a few words of wisdom to his son — Kwi-wi-sens (or "Boy"). When he died, he was buried according to his instructions on Baldur Bluff — overlooking the Mississippi. Here, in death, he continued his vigil for the canoes of the Sioux.

Carl Zapffe tells us in his book, "The Man Who Lived in Three Centuries," that in 1971, when the Little Falls-Brainerd-Staples area was deluged by the greatest cloudburst of recorded times—washing out sections of Highway #10 and the Burlington Northern Railroad tracks and isolating northern Minnesota for more than a day—many recalled the "legend of Hole-in-the-Day's promise."

Major Lawrence Taliaferro, the Indian agent who founded Eatonville.

Courtesy Library of Congress

Shortly before his fateful trip to St. Paul, he is said to have prophesied his death and promised that if he were buried on this high bluff, his spirit would brood over the area and protect it from storms. According to meteorological record, the area near his burial place was free from any tornadoes or devastating storms until the 1971 deluge. Interestingly enough, it was in that year that new highway construction came within fifty yards of the granite stone that marks his grave. Was the spirit of Hole-in-the-Day warning that his resting place must not be disturbed???

Hole-in-the-Day was described by the whitemen who knew him as tall, handsome and athletic. He was a charismatic leader of his people, an orator and a brave warrior. Both he and his son, Hole-in-the-Day the Younger, may be thought of as scoundrels by the standards of today's culture, but when judged by the culture of their time, they must be characterized as outstanding leaders of their people who had major impact not only on the history of Gull Lake but also on the history of the State of Minnesota.

Kwi-wi-sens (Boy) becomes Hole-in-the-Day II

With the passing of his father, Kwi-wi-sens ("Boy") became the principal chief of the Gull Lake and Crow Wing Ojibwe. He took his father's

name as his own and we remember him as Chief Hole-in-the-Day II (or "the younger") – the last of the major Ojibwe chiefs. That is not to say that great Ojibwe leadership has not followed, but after Hole-in-the-Day the power base was gone, Indian lands had been signed away in treaty after treaty and the rout of the Sioux in 1862 left white man clearly in control of Minnesota and the destiny of the American Indian.

Hole-in-the-Day had headquarters at both the mouth of the Crow Wing and at his boyhood home on Gull Lake. It is believed that the log cabin located at Highway 371 and the Mission Road was his (later, Chief Wadena's). He also

Courtesy of the Minnesota Historical Society

Chief Hole-in-the-Day, the Younger. He cut a wide swath across the pages of 19th century Ojibwe history.

built a cabin several hundred yards east of his father's earlier home in Ojibwe Park—between Round and Long Lakes.

Hole-in-the-Day's followers inhabited the parcel of land bordered by Round, Long and Gull Lakes. The Treaty of 1864 gave Hole-in-the-Day personally one square mile of land in this area including the site for his house.

Old Hole-in-the-Day had raised "Boy" to be tough, hard, and aggressive. When a lad not yet in his teens (1838), his father "arranged" for him to stab and scalp a Sioux girl of about the same age.

By 1855, Hole-in-the-Day II at age 27, was recognized by the whites as the principal chief of the Gull Lake-Crow Wing Ojibwe—and was so designated in the treaty signed that year establishing the Gull Lake reservation. This action was not well received by all Ojibwe. Kwi-wi-sens-ish or "Bad Boy," was sufficiently disgruntled to leave Gull and take up residence at Mille Lacs Lake (along with his followers). As mentioned earlier,

Hole-in-the-Day didn't care for Bad Boy either, because the latter turned in three Indian murderers to white authorities. He threatened to kill him on several occasions.

Hole-in-the-Day II got the attention of Territorial Governor Ramsey and most Minnesotans in 1850 when he and a small party (perhaps only one or two others) attacked six Sioux (taking one scalp) just across the river from St. Paul (after hiding in the gorge of Fountain Cave). The attack was probably in reprisal for the Sioux annihilation of a party of fifteen Ojibwe a little more than a month earlier on the Apple River in Wisconsin. Governor Ramsey summoned the chiefs of both the Sioux and the Ojibwe to a peace council at Fort Snelling. On June 9th, Hole-in-the-Day arrived with about 100 braves; late the following morning about 300 Sioux arrived on horseback; they dismounted in a display of pageantry and saluted the Ojibwe who had lined up to welcome them. Governor Ramsey presided personally at the council. William Warren, the Ojibwe historian whom we have quoted earlier, read the charges against the Sioux, and Bad Hail read the counter-charges against the Ojibwe. All sides finally agreed to abide by the provisions of the treaty of 1843 and the council concluded with a feast.

Earlier in the proceedings the Sioux Chiefs had left the council in protest of the presence of some white women who were on hand as members of the Governor's party. Hole-in-the-Day II scored a coup by offering the women seats among his people. However, the women thought it best to leave, and when the Sioux returned they were sharply taken to task by Governor Ramsey. But the council concluded peacefully and to the satisfaction of the Governor, but mistrust on both sides was still evident as hostages were required to insure safe journeys home.

Battle of Bloody Cove

Oral history tells us that the Ojibwe thwarted many attempts by the Dakotas to reclaim Gull Lake. On one occasion the Dakota Sioux were annihilated in a bloody conflict at this site.

Gull Lake during the Civil War

Attempts were made to draw the Minnesota Ojibwe into the Civil War on the side of the north. John Johnson whose Indian name was Enmegahbowh (the one who stands before his people), as mentioned earlier, served as a deacon of the Episcopal Mission (St. Columba) on Gull Lake. He reported that a man named Horn, a whisky trader, tried to recruit Ojibwe warriors for Fort Snelling, where they would become union soldiers. Johnson said that he was asked by Horn to help him recruit braves from Mille Lacs Lake; he refused. Horn reportedly paid between

Courtesy of the Minnesota Historical Society

Chief Little Crow in 1858–general of the great Sioux uprising in 1862.

fifty and two hundred dollars as a "signing bonus" — which in most cases was spent on Horn's whisky before the braves reached the fort.

Fathers of some of the Leech Lake warriors who had been recruited were so upset they came to Gull Lake looking for Horn with the intent to kill him. Johnson persuaded the fathers to hold off while he made a trip to Fort Snelling to try to stop the practice. He approached Henry Rice (one of our two first U.S. Senators) and Commandant Henry Sibley. The latter said he was unaware of the practice and promised to put a stop to it. When Johnson reported this back to the fathers, they were satisfied and returned to Leech Lake.

Dakota Sioux and Ojibwe Uprisings in 1862

When our Civil war broke out, the American Indian was anxious, puzzled, and tempted. He had seen white man's governments topple before. The British had replaced the French and the American "Long Knives" had replaced the British and in 1812 the British had threatened to reclaim their lost ground. Was the Great White Father in Washington on the way out? White civilization had not given the Indian much cause to rejoice; if there would ever be an opportunity to reclaim his old lands and rid the area of the white man—it was then.

The Minnesota Sioux seemed less fearful of white man as a result of the Civil War. The Ojibwe were not so sure, but Hole-in-the-Day II was apparently ready to take a chance. Historians do not agree whether or not there was collaboration between these age-old rival tribes, but there is evidence that Chiefs Little Crow and Hole-in-the-Day II conspired while they were together at Fort Snelling. In his letters to Nathan Richardson of Little Falls, John Johnson (Enmegahbowh) stated that Hole-in-the-Day had received a message from Little Crow which invited the Ojibwe to join the fight against the whites.

At any rate, both tribes went on the offense on the very same day, on August 18, 1862, when the Sioux and the Ojibwe swung into action more than one hundred miles apart. The simultaneous attacks were supposedly timed for the middle day of the three-day dark of the moon period which occurs monthly—when there is no moon at all, all night long. Hole-in-the-Day attack St. Columbo Mission and Little Crow attack the white settlers in the New Ulm area.

There was at least one important difference in the two attacks—Little Crow had the support of the vast majority of his people; Hole-in-the-Day controlled only the Gull Lake-Crow Wing area. He had been in communication, however, with the Ojibwe at Leech Lake, Battle Lake and elsewhere and thought he could count on their support. If he had been correct in his assumption, northern Minnesota would have been subjected to the same bloodbath as the Minnesota River Valley. As it was, southern

Minnesota became the setting for the most devastating massacre in the nation's history. This atrocity, plus the annihilation of Custer and his men at Little Big Horn and the culmination of whiteman's reprisals at Wounded Knee, taken together, are the most deplorable chapter in the history of white-Indian relations.

As with all wars, there were direct causes or incidents which triggered the fighting and then the more significant indirect causes. Let us examine the latter, first. The Indians had many reason for dissatisfaction and concern: (1) there was an obvious westward movement of whites with a ravenous hunger for land; (2) Indian policies of the United States Government were disheartening—treaty payments were late and meager. Indian Agents were political appointees, often ill prepared for their jobs, and the Indians were literally compressed into reservations; and (3) the very nature of the Sioux people, at least at that time, was warlike and aggressive and they were not accustomed to being pushed around without fighting back.

The incident that triggered this war was the killing of five whites by four Wahpeton braves on the farm of Howard Baker near Acton. Understanding the significance of the murders, the Sioux debated long into the night what course of action to take. Tradition holds that Little Crow opposed further violence against the whites, comparing the white soldiers who would come for revenge to "clouds of grasshoppers."

Some believe that Little Crow yielded to his hot-blooded braves in fear that they would turn elsewhere for leadership. They had already turned not long before to another chief called "Traveling Hail" for "chief speaker." And so the die was cast and the balance of the night was spent in preparation for attack. The next day, August 18, 1862, Little Crow lead about two hundred warriors against the Redwood Indian Agency. Victory came easily.

There is every evidence that the whites of Minnesota were completely surprised by the uprising. Frontier newspapers of the day gave no indication of immediate concern, even though it was common knowledge that the treaty payments due the Indians were long overdue.

Sioux victories came quickly following the success at the Lower Agency; (1) of forty-six soldiers who followed Captain John Marsh out of Fort Ridgely on their way to Redwood, more than half, including the captain, perished; (2) more than fifty members of German farm families in Brown and Nicollet Counties were also killed on the first day; (3) New Ulm was attacked twice — but survived[6]; (4) more than eight hundred Sioux lay siege to Fort Ridgely — but the fort held; and (5) at the ambush at Birch Coulee, more than eighty soldiers were killed. Estimates ran as high as five hundred[7] whites killed and a thousand wounded; the number of Indian casualties remains unknown. But in a matter of weeks it was all over.

Sibley amassed an army of more than 1600 men; many more were in reserve. Sheer numbers made it just a matter of time until the Sioux would have to accept the futility of their uprising. The Battle of Wood Lake was fought on September 23. Although a massive action, only seven soldiers were killed or died later as a result. There was a futile Sioux attack on Fort Abercrombie a few days later, followed by isolated skirmishes, but the war was over. Little Crow and his surviving warriors fled to the Dakotas and Canada. The Battle of Little Big Horn and the tragedy of Wounded Knee were yet to come, along with dozens of smaller skirmishes, but for Minnesotans there would be only one more armed clash between whites and Indians – and that would be at Leech Lake thirty-six years later.[8]

As an aftermath to the war, more than 300 Sioux prisoners were condemned to death. Because of the huge number, Sibley decided to share the burden of decision by referring the final judgment to General Pope. The general, in turn, passed it on to that desk "where the buck always stops"–to President Lincoln, himself. Even though already heavily burdened by the great Civil War, President Lincoln ordered a review of each case, individually, and expressed his desire that no man should die merely because he participated in the war. Only those who had murdered civilians or were guilty of rape (just two cases) were to pay with their lives. It is said that in the end, Lincoln personally reviewed the history of each man he sentenced to death. On his written order, thirty-eight Sioux warriors were hanged, simultaneously, in Mankato on December 26, 1862.

Following the uprising a $500 price was placed on Little Crow's head and the state paid bounties for Sioux scalps. Little Crow returned to Minnesota with a few braves and was killed by a hunting party near Hutchinson. The reward was collected by Nathan Lawson. His body was identified by his deformed hands and wrists, the result of a quarrel with his brothers over who would become chief following the death of his father. He became the third "Little Crow" of his tribe. When the bullet had passed through his wrists, he had gone to Fort Snelling for help. The surgeon suggested amputation, Little Crow decided to gamble and with the help of his own medicine man and "mother nature," he was able to use his hands. He was killed on July 3, 1863. The next day his body was dragged through the streets of Hutchinson as part of the July 4th celebration and finally cast on the city dump. Later he was buried in St. Paul. More than 100 years later he was re-buried by the Big Sioux River near Flandreau, So. Dakota.

As Little Crow was leading the Dakotas against the Redwood Agency, Hole-in-the-Day II was at the very same time directing the obliteration of the St. Cloumba Mission on Gull Lake by several hundred Ojibwe warriors who had been gathered from as far as Sandy Lake to the east and Ottertail on the west. Why did the wily Chieftain choose the little church on the shores of Gull Lake as the subject of his first attack when he could have chosen strategic Fort Ripley or the white settlers of Crow Wing? First of all, the mission not only symbolized white man but it also represented his foreign religion. Secondly, Hole-in-the-Day may have been waiting for the expected reinforcements from Leech Lake. If, in truth, there was collaboration between the Sioux and the Ojibwe, he may have felt compelled to do something dramatic on the agreed day but did not want to risk defeat at another location while he was waiting for substantial reinforcements.

The burning of the mission was a cheap victory. The white clergy had been frightened away from the work at Gull Lake five years earlier in 1857 and had left it in the care of Enmegahbowh. The faithful Ottawa Indian and his family had taken flight by canoe to Crow Wing and then Fort Ripley the night before the attack.

Flush with the satisfaction of the successful completion of his act of defiance, Hole-in-the-Day was reported to have been anxious for the arrival of the Leech Lake Ojibwe so he could proceed with his planned attack against the reservation agency, the village of Crow Wing, Fort Ripley, St. Cloud and—perhaps— on to join forces with the Sioux. But the leadership of the Leech Lake bands were having second thoughts. The younger warriors, eager for battle, had quickly taken the few whites in the area into captivity and proposed a public execution. However, two respected chiefs, Buffalo and Big Dog, were not so sure Hole-in-the-Day II would be the eventual victor. Wisely they persuaded their braves to bring the captives to Gull Lake, reasoning that if Hole-in-the-Day had changed his mind or had not been successful, the Leech Lake Indians would be left alone to feel the wrath of the whites. After a two day journey, they arrived at the appointed rendezvous between Round Lake and Gull Lake. Encouraged by the reinforcements, Hole-in-the-Day decided to attack the Indian Agency, located on the Gull River where it enters the Crow Wing.

John Johnson (Enmegahbowh) in his letters to Nathan Richardson, (a Little Falls judge and history buff) describes what happened:

I stayed at Gull Lake Mission. All the white missionaries had deserted me and had gone to the congenial country for their coward spirits. I understood that the warriors were proposing to attack the Agency. When I heard this, I yoked up my horned horses to flee away to Crow Wing. I started in the early part of the night. When I had gone about half way, in the morning, four warriors overtook us and said I must return home, and that no harm would be done us. Here I was with my wife and children undecided what course to take. My wife advised me to return home. When we arrived home Hole-in-the-Day came to see us and said that we must not be alarmed, and that no harm would be done us.

In the course of a few days, Chief Crossing Sky of Rabbit Lake came to my house in the darkest hour of the night, and said, "I am come to advise you to prepare to flee away to Fort Ripley. Hole-in-the-Day is going to march with his warriors to the Agency in two days from today and massacre all the whites. Be sure to flee away. For when he returns he will be so ugly and spare no one whom he knows has sympathy with the whites."

The chief went out. My wife cried, and said, "The people, then, must be informed what is coming upon them. If I cannot find anyone to bear the news I will go. There is no time to lose."

The time was short; but is so happened that a white man came in late in the evening to ask me what was the meaning of so much drumming and so many war whoops. I told him all about it, and urged him to carry my letter to the people of the Agency, that they may be preparing shelter or a strong stockade for their defense. For a long time he would not go. He was very fearful. I said to him, "The Indians will find out you are here with me and will kill you. If you cannot go, my wife will go." At last with much fear he started away with my message. This poor man's name was Yankknight. You must have known him, for he lived at Crow Wing for many years.

Sure enough, one Saturday afternoon Hole-in-the-Day and his warriors passed through near my door, naked and painted black all over his body and singing the war songs. My wife cried after the warriors had passed away out of sight. I said to her that I apprehended no danger for the people there, for they must have received my letter and have had plenty of time to prepare them a strong stockade. When they received my letter both the women and children worked like beavers.

Hole-in-the-Day with his warriors arrived at the Agency and halted a quarter of a mile away. It was about morning or before daybreak. He sent two warriors to go and see whether any preparation had been made against being attacked. To their great astonishment they find that an old heavy log house, built by the soldiers years ago, strongly, with heavy logs, was now full of lights. and all around the building were port holes, and each port hole contained two or three guns well loaded.

About a month before this several boxes of guns arrived at the Agency. From the beginning and for many years, the government had given them guns and ammunition with their annual payments. The guns had arrived and the doomed people opened the boxes, and had plenty of ammunition to use to shoot the hearts of the Indians.

The spies returned to bear the message to Hole-in-the-Day and told him that the people were well fortified, and it was of no use to attack them, for "before we can kill one single white squaw, many of us will be *shot down and caused to kiss the dust. They have been warned what was coming upon them."*

Hole-in-the-Day jumped up with vengeance of exasperation and said "Let us return home. I know the treacherous man who gave the information. Enmegahbowh is the man. He shall surely die and just as soon as we reach home. The first thing I shall do is go to his house and shoot him down like a dog. Mark you" said he to his warriors, "all of you shall see me doing it, and shall bear witness to the act."

At this time I was safely housed and protected in the hands of the government soldiers. Sure enough when Hole-in-the-Day and his party arrived at home and came opposite my house he halted and with his loaded gun started to go to my house. He found that I had gone to some place. He said again, "He must die. I shall not let him go. I shall find him where he has fled."

Until his death, Hole-in-the-Day continued to threaten John Johnson, but so far as we know never did actually try to kill him.

Following Hole-in-the-Day's aborted attack, Major Walker, the local Indian agent, fled to Fort Ripley. He did not stay there long because he feared its meager defenses would not withstand an attack by Hole-in-the-Day's forces. He headed for Fort Snelling and on his way met the U.S. Commissioner for Indian Affairs, William Dole, in the village of t. Cloud. He told him that Indian forces were about to attack Fort Ripley and that in his opinion the whites didn't have a chance. Dole then contacted Governor Ramsey and persuaded him to send 300 soldiers to protect the fort.

Meanwhile, Walker continued his journey to Fort Snelling along with a handful of "halfbreeds" for his protection. His body was later found by Big Lake. He had been shot in the head, apparently with his own gun. The protectors were gone; so were all his valuables. It has never been definitely decided whether his death was suicide or homicide.

Oua-wi-sain-shish (Bad Boy). He may have been "Bad Boy" to Hole-in-the-Day but he was a hero to the whites of central Minnesota.

Courtesy Crow Wing County Historical Society.

Dole sent word to Hole-in-the-Day to come to Fort Ripley to talk. The chief refused but agreed to meet at Crow Wing. The talks resolved nothing but the whites gained time. Hole-in-the-Day retreated to Gull River, above the agency. Dole had made it very clear that if the Ojibwe attack the whites they would receive no money or goods—ever—from the United States Government.

Father Pierz and George Sweet of the little village of St. Cloud approached Hole-in-the-Day and tried to reason with him, but perhaps the biggest factor in breaking the stalemate was Chief Bad Boy's decision to join the whites against his rival chief. Bad Boy and his braves marched on Fort Ripley—but not to wage war as was first thought by the panic stricken settlers—but rather to offer support and, if necessary, join in battle against Hole-in-the-Day. Further, he sent a messenger directly to the Gull Lake chieftain advising him of his decision. Hole-in-the-Day may have been a lot of things, but he was not stupid. Reluctantly, but wisely, he permitted the abortion of the campaign.

If Hole-in-the-Day II had been successful in organizing all of the Ojibwe and had proceeded with his original plans and perhaps even joined forces with the Sioux, it would have only postponed the inevitable white victory for a little while, but thousands, instead of hundreds, of whites and Indians would have perished.

After the 1862 affair, Hole-in-the-Day lived out his relatively short life surrounded by his people in the triangle of land between Gull, Long and Round Lakes, and at Crow Wing. He had a comfortable cabin designed white-man style.

Major Cullen, the Indian agent after Walker, described Hole-in-the-Day's circumstances to the St. Paul Pioneer and Democrat thus:

> *Chief Hole-in-the-Day has built himself a gay old house on his reserved 640 acres at Crow Wing on the Mississippi River. The house has cost him $6,000 in gold and is nearly surrounded by a piazza. The chief is living with six wives in all the splendor of a Mormon Bishop. His parlor is furnished with 17 rocking chairs, while the walls are hung with 8 large portraits, seven of which represent himself, and the other Major Cullen. They live like white folks, all sit at the same table and have the best china and coffee sets for every day use. He has over one hundred acres of his reserve under cultivation which brings forth bountifully. His wives work a large garden well stocked with flowers.*

When Hole-in-the-Day backed down after the soldier reinforcements arrived at Fort Ripley and Chief Bad Boy threatened to join the whites, a few settlers were brave enough to burn down his house at Crow Wing. When Hole-in-the-Day agreed to be peaceful, the U.S. Government gave him $5,000 to build a new home and title to the square mile of land where it would be located (Treaty of 1864). The Treaty of 1867 assured Hole-in-the-Day he would continue to receive the $1,000 per year promised his father in the Treaty of 1848.

The Exodus

The 1867 Treaty also provided for a new reservation at White Earth (Mahnomen) and the Gull Lake – Crow Wing Ojibwe were told to move there. Nearly all of them did, but over Hole-in-the-Day's objections. Even though he had signed the treaty, he did all he could to discourage his people from going there. The fact that nearly all of the people did go to White Earth indicates the chief had lost much of his power. John Johnson (Enmegahbowh) in his letters to Judge Nathan Richardson of Little Falls tells it this way:

The chiefs and the old men and women often come and ask if I knew anything about their removal. I said out openly, "Yes, I think that very thing must come to affect us, because the government has and is still removing the different Indian tribes all over the United States, for some cause, a good cause. It is always a good cause, because the government makes it to become such. Here it is. Just see it. Bye-and-bye, I say, you all shall be removed. Now if you ask me why, if you have done anything to justify your removal, look back a year ago. See what you have done, and the warriors who came and were ready to make a general warfare against your friends the whites. My friends, had I not been a living man, mark you, when you started to go on with the warfare, had I not interfered, today all you people would not have walked on your beautiful ground nor paddled your canoes on these beautiful lakes and rivers. You would have been destroyed and swept away from the face of the earth. And for saving you and interfering, you wanted to kill me, and you would have done it had I not escaped from my home you would have killed me. In doing the above I showed my love toward you. You are all here, smoking your pipe of peace. You ought to thank me for it. And for this very foolish act of yours the government will say to you all you must remove."

Sure enough, on the next year following the most dreadful word reached the ears of my people. "You must be removed toward the setting sun, near to the country of your great heredity enemies." To describe the feelings and sayings of my people would fill many sheets of paper. I will pass them over and will give you a few items that actually occurred. Hole-in-the-Day took up against the cause, and advised his people not to move. He was very bitter against it, and even threatened death to the first man who would not give heed to his words. He must surely die. The day was named on which they must be ready to move. Hole-in-the-Day got ready, and sent four of his best warriors to the road to watch and intercept the first man who may pass and to halt him. The warriors started to do as they were commanded. Chief Turtle or Na-bun-a-skong were to lead the caravan. He was considered one of the bravest and most daring warriors. He walked ahead of the moving caravan, feathers waving on his head, and singing the war song. Here were Hole-in-the-Day's braves watching the moving caravan come on, two of the braves standing on each side of the road. Sure enough, here came the moving caravan, and Chief Na-bun-a-skong saw them watching. When he saw them standing on both sides of the road, he made a loud war whoop, as much as to say, "I, too, am a brave and warrior!" Everybody thought it would cause much trouble and bloodshed; and as the chief was nearing them, and passing, he thought he would be shot down every moment. But he passed through without any effort on their part to stop him. After the first move took place, Hole-in-the-Day saw that his work was not heeded nor noticed. He gave up the cause; and yet there was one more item that he will never overlook, and that he must attend to himself, personally, and without fail, and that is to make his final settlement with Enmegahbowh, the treacherous man.

Thus the removal took place without any trouble. My poor people have gone away broken hearted. I pitied the poor women most, and felt much sympathy for them. I never can forget what Na-bun-a-skong did before his final step took place for the unknown country. Looking at the deep pine forest, with his hands stretched forth, and with a deep voice he said, "O you majestic pine forest, how often have I sought shelter and protection under thy great wing! Thy songs have often cheered me and thy waving heads have halted me to listen to thy melodious songs. Oh, you majestic pine forest! Continue to sing thy beautiful songs, to awaken and to cheer my dear children that I have left behind me in their graves!" Turning toward the Mississippi and pointing to it he said, "Oh, ye, the father of rivers, for ages past thy beautiful current has often cheered while gliding over thy currents with my canoe! I am leaving thee! I shall never again grace thy flowing waters. I leave thee, not by my wish, but I am compelled." And again pointing towards the mountain, he said, with a loud voice, "Oh, you beautiful mount! How often have I hidden under thy walls when in danger!" So saying he returned, much cast down and with spirits of melancholy. He was the most earnest advocate that I should move with them. But, at the same time, he knew well that it was not safe for me to move with them when the loaded gun was pointed at me. Again and again I said that the Great Spirit would open the door for me to enter into their country.

Because the Mille Lacs Lake Ojibwe had stood up to Hole-in-the-Day and offered to help protect the whites, they were allowed to stay on their lake and were even promised more land.

The Treaty of 1867, which provided for the removal of the Gull Lake Ojibwe to White Earth, was the last to effect the Gull Lake area. For the record, it should be noted that there were four earlier treaties:

1847 – with Hole-in-the-Day I, giving permission to log the area.

1855 – ceded a large area around Gull Lake to the United States and established the Gull Lake reservation with an agency on the Gull River six miles above Crow Wing (the community). D.B. Herriman was the first agent. There were four buildings.

1863 – provided for a transfer of a large amount of land around Gull, Mille Lacs, Sandy, Rabbit and other lakes to the United States in exchange for a reservation near Cass and Leech Lakes. Objections raised by the Ojibwe resulted in the treaty not being consummated.

1864 – provided for the Leech-Cass reservations but allowed Gull and Mille Lacs bands to stay where they were and gave Hole-in-the-Day $5,000 for the loss of his home.

The Murder of Chief Hole-in-the-Day II

Hole-in-the-Day II was only about 40 years of age when he was murdered on a trail along Gull River on July 9, 1868. Although it is known that he was shot by a small group of nine Ojibwe from Leech Lake, the motive is unclear. Some historians believe that it was murder for hire. Surely Hole-in-the-Day had his share of enemies, both Indian and white. A group of Ojibwe from Wisconsin who were living at Crow Wing were particularly unhappy with Hole-in-the-Day because he insisted they were not eligible to move to White Earth. We have no record of the killers being punished. There was one witness, another local Ojibwe who was traveling with him; he was allowed to live. Hole-in-the-Day was buried in a Catholic cemetery in Crow Wing.

At the time of his death, Hole-in-the-Day was living with five wives – three were Ojibwe, one was a Sioux and another was white. He had met the latter in 1867 when he was in Washington, D.C. negotiating a treaty. She worked at the hotel where he stayed. He married her and brought her back to his home at Gull Lake. It is unfortunate that there is no record of what her impressions were of this foreign setting! After Hole-in-the-Day's death, the white woman moved to Minneapolis and found work; she took her young son (by Hole-in-the-Day) with her. The child was adopted by a family named Woodbury and he took that name; his first name was John.

The Sioux wife was so upset when Hole-in-the-Day brought home a white woman that she moved out, along with her son. She had been the chief's favorite. Legend has it that she finally committed suicide by jumping off Dutchman's Bluff.

The first white owner of Hole-in-the-Day's property was Anton Mahlum of Brainerd. He purchased it from the chief's heirs in 1899.

The End of the 100 Years Dakota-Ojibwe War

There were dozens of other battles between the Dakotas and the Ojibwe which are not included here because they did not occur near Gull Lake or involve villagers of that lake.[8]

The 100 Years War came to an end because the white military forces drove the Sioux out of the state during the 1862 uprising. The next year (1863) the military marched into the Dakotas and most of the Sioux fled farther west or north into Canada.

With a few minor exceptions, the Ojibwe were the only Native American people left in Minnesota; there was no one to fight. Relatively small numbers of Sioux eventually returned to the state. At this writing, the Dakotas operate very profitable casinos at Shakopee, Red Wing and Morton.

We cannot even venture a guess as to how many Dakotas and Ojibwe lost their lives during the century-long conflict. Surely there were thousands—men, women, and even children. It was the practice of both the Dakotas and the Ojibwe to kill everyone, hoping to totally eliminate their enemies. We can only imagine the pain and suffering endured by families as individuals were killed — not to mention those wounded and maimed. Sometimes whole villages were obliterated.

Tragically, as with most wars, it was all for naught; nothing really changed. From the ousting of the Dakotas from the woodlands in 1766 to the end of the conflict in 1862, the Dakotas did not take back one inch of the Minnesota woodlands, nor were the Ojibwe able to expand their territory into the prairies. In more than 100 years of fighting, nothing was gained; everyone lost.

Footnotes

[1] It was believed by some that if one were scalped, that is how he/she would appear in the hereafter.

[2] Waub-o-jeeg was a sub chief of the next generation; his village was located at the base of Gull (Squaw) Point. He guarded the strategic outlet of the lake.

[3] Nicollet called Long Lake "Sibley" in honor of the man who led the state militia at Fort Snelling during the Civil War and who later became Governor of Minnesota.

[4] Firm Ground and Hole-in-the-Day's family lived on Lake Superior. Evidently they were in the Leech Lake or Gull Lake area when Flat Mouth and Curly Head organized their attack on the Long Prairie Sioux.

[5] John Smith was a Cass Lake Ojibwe who was well over 100 years old when he died and actually did live in three centuries.

[6] More than 90 buildings were burned, some by the whites in defense of the city.

[7] Four hundred and eighty-six is the figure accepted by most historians today.

[8] For further information about the conflict, read "Indian Wars" by this author.

CHAPTER IV

Missionary Efforts

Explorers came to North America for fame and adventure. Traders were interested in profit. But the missionaries were interested in bringing the Good News of the Gospel to the American Indians. The handful of God's servants who unselfishly and courageously worked among the Minnesota Indians and white settlers in the 17th, 18th, and 19th centuries have never received the full credit they deserved for the role they played in the development of our state and nation. Their letters and diaries reveal the agonies and anxieties they suffered. They realized they might very well be called on to even give their lives; and Father Alneau did in the Lake of the Woods massacre.

Among these spiritual giants was the Reverend James Lloyd Breck, Episcopal clergyman, who established the St. Columba Mission on the southern shores of Gull Lake in 1852. His work was relatively encouraging, but he was attracted to the larger population of Ojibwe on Leech Lake and moved there in November of 1856. But here he met frustration and bitter disappointment. He described the Pillagers as "so drunk and disorderly" that his efforts were in vain. He gave up his work only eight months after his arrival and actually left in fear of his life. Other missionaries did come to Leech Lake including the Rev. Charles T. Wright, an Indian from Gull Lake and son of chief Waub-o-jeeg.

When Breck transferred his efforts to Leech Lake, other missionaries including a Rev. Pike, apparently carried on the work for a few months, but Breck's Ottawa assistant, John Johnson (Enmegahbowh), ended up in charge. He was both dedicated and capable and fulfilled his duties until the night before the burning of the mission by Hole-in-the-Day's army. He was later ordained a priest and continued his work among the Ojibwe at White Earth.

While the missionaries were at St. Columba, they reached out to the Indians in the Gull Lake area. Tradition has it that the Ojibwe at the south end of the lake were served through meetings held at Mission Point —

St. Columba Mission of Gull Lake, sketched in 1852. It was Hole-in-the-Day's first target.

First Episcopal Convert at Gull Lake, 1852.
Rev. J. Lloyd Breck at the right and Rev. En-me-gah-bowh (John Johnson) at the left.

hence the name. Madden's Resort is located on this point. (The St. Columba site is also called Mission Point.)

In an incident related to the destruction of the St. Columba mission, a Lutheran church on Mission lake (located several miles east of Gull) was also burned in 1862. The church had been built where a small creek flows from Lower Mission to the Mississippi. The Lutheran pastor, Ron Ottomar Cloetter, then established a mission at Crow Wing.

By returning to John Johnson's letters to Nathan Richardson, we can get a first hand account of his experiences when he arrived at the White Earth Reservation.

And here is another question. These chiefs and warriors were all heathen. They worshipped to wood and stone. They go to meet a man who comes with a different religious spirit, a man who comes to destroy and annihilate their religious faith and worship, the grand medicine faith of our forefathers and great grandfathers. This man, Enmegahbowh, came to teach them a new religion. (Some of these chiefs had heard my teaching before they were removed). What changed them, and caused they to grasp the Christian teachings?

The first night of our encampment shall never be forgotten. We were talking and talking about our future, what to do and how to live in the new country, White Earth. I was so glad to hear them. I did not at once urge upon them that they all must turn to Christianity. This very point I leave until I know the favorable time has arrived. Our encampment four nights were spent talking of our great aim to raise them from their present condition. On the fourth day all left me to go home and bear the message that the poor Enmegahbowh was coming sure, and would be there in two days. And this made no little stir with gladness. But there was one, an educated mixed blood, who was opposed to my coming, and he told the heathen that I was coming to do much injury to them and to their new country. The chiefs and warriors gave no heed, and his foolish talking did not amount to much of anything.

I arrived on Friday. A little comfortable log house had been provided for my dwelling house. Sunday came, and to my great astonishment, chiefs and headmen, women and children, of all grades, came to listen to my teachings. I was moved with compassion to see them seek shelter and strong stockade for shelter, the most impregnable fortress of Christian religion, the only hope of salvation for my unfortunate race.

My greatest aim was to catch all the leading chiefs and to kill all their little hope that was in them, because when this is done and accomplished, I shall think that my work is truly commenced. This had truly come to pass. I have never seen so much earnestness manifested by these chiefs, talking and talking to their people to receive my instructions, the only hope of our people and of their welfare.

During the winter we used the largest wigwam or log house, and during the summer I held my public services under the shade of the trees. In the second year I had nearly all the chiefs and the leading men and women and children under my teachings. I must say I have lived with my own people from the beginning of my days to the present time. I never saw so large a community of heathen people live so harmoniously and in so great peace. It was like one family. O, those early days of yore! I long to see and enjoy their blessings. At that early day we had no Devil spirit nor anything to make us dumb and crazy. We loved and helped one another. I have often remarked to my wife that I was in a new world, and with new human beings. My joy was full, and I had plenty to give away to others. Thus, my dear Mr. Richardson, the whole work moved on harmoniously and in great peace, for there was nothing to interrupt nor impede our enterprises until the Devil spirit entered into our peaceful abodes. Drunkenness put on all their garb, and beautiful she pretended to be, but she soon demolished and impeded our whole work. The various species of human beings began to arrive and our efforts began to slacken and be impeded. Before this I had the biggest chieftain under my instruction. As I have remarked already the head chief, White Cloud, came to my house and said, "Enmegahbowh, my brother-in-law, I came to make known what is in my heart. We are very near the country of our great enemies, the Sioux nation. Several months ago the Pillager Indians went over not very far from us, and killed a whole family and scalped them. I shall expect them to make retaliation, or perhaps they are preparing to make a great war against us. Several of us chiefs and head warriors propose to go to the Sioux country to try to make peace with them, and on reaching their country we will leave our guns behind us and go to grasp their hands without any war implements about us. The great enemies, seeing us without arms shall be fully convinced that our hearts are fully prepared to make peace, a permanent peace, not for one month or year; but for all time to come. I know it is a great risk and a great venture of faith. Now, dear brother-in-law, why should I propose this great undertaking, a dangerous and uncertain path for reaching the object sought for? My heart has been greatly changed from deep seated hatred to loving my enemies. My fathers and myself even, have worshipped to the Unknown God, yes, even to wood and stone. Today my people have turned their hearts to the living God and are worshipping Him, I hope with true hearts. It is under His great protection I propose to visit my enemies. I am confident to reach the lands of my enemies without anything happening to me. God is my hope and my trust and I shall go with these staffs."

I said, "Now my dear friend, it is a great risk and a great undertaking and the words you have spoken are the true armor and are worth more than one hundred of the best warriors. Yes, God knows that we have been wandering through the various ways, here and there, without God and without hope in the world. Our country was taken away from you. You became shipwrecked like an orphan without a father to guide and protect you, and finally you were moved away from your bondage of sin and misery to seek a far country, and through your wanderings you have at last found a country, White Earth, where honey and milk flow. Here you are almost bewildered, and at last begin a new life in a new country. The poor Enmegahbowh arrived. He commenced to give you instruction and said to you all, my friends, please let me tell you what is true, and then invited you, saying, why halt ye between two opinions? If the Great God be God, serve him, or if Baal be God, serve him. Dear friends, you have heeded it, and taken my instructions, and have become true worshipers of the true and living God. Yes, dear friends go, go! God, whom you have trusted and worshipped, will guide and protect you to accomplish the great work; and peace and harmony shall be perpetuated all the days of your lives."

Again he said, "I shall be gone ten days. In ten days I shall be back to see you all again if nothing happens to me."

On the following day the chiefs with their warriors started away to the country of their great enemies. Nine days passed away and tomorrow was the day appointed for their return home. During the eight night hardly anyone slept to await the ninth day. The ninth day came. My people, both men and women, stirred together. Here and there a group of men and women were standing toward afternoon. No appearance of our men was seen. Late in the night the men and women retired to their home, and on the next day the men and women again appeared on the same watch ground where they were waiting yesterday. Again they were disappointed as they were yesterday. No one came. Toward the evening the people began to feel uneasy about their friends. On the third day when no friend appeared, they became hopeless and despaired. They thought their friends must have been killed surely. On the fourth day my people came in to ask me what I thought about our friends. I said with a confident tone, in my great faith, "My friends, do not become hopeless. I know that they are all still living, and we shall soon see them coming home all safe. I say this, the Great Spirit will not forsake them in time of their danger. He knows them, and they trusted in Him. And besides, their work is great, and He will assist them to do it and to accomplish it." This talk relieved them greatly and on the fifth day some one took a walk a long distance toward the road our friends took when they started away from us. He brought the word that he heard guns fired a long distance away toward the path our friends took.

The news soon spread to the whole settlement, and the people began to gather waiting for someone to arrive. In about three hours our friends appeared upon a hill and began to fire their guns. Men and women, even children ran toward them, to shake hands with them, singing the song of peace for what they have accomplished. Here was large gathering of men, women and children. The friends came and shook hands with me heartily, and with much joy and peace.

Thus, Hon. N. Richardson, you can see and understand what the Christian Indian had accomplished, a permanent peace and forever.

John Johnson was evidently far more successful in converting Native Americans to Christianity than were the white missionaries. This seems to have also been true in other parts of the country as well.

CHAPTER V

The Fur Trade

Eighteenth and nineteenth century Europeans had a tremendous appetite for furs. Anyone who was anybody in European society wore fur hats and coats in winter. The French and English colonies in North America were the major sources for these furs. The demand was so great that the east coast of the continent was soon trapped out. As early as 1670, with the chartering of the Hudson's Bay Company by Charles I of England, fur trading posts were established in new locations nearer the center of the continent. Radisson and Groseilliers, both of French descent and organizers of the England based Hudson's Bay Company, penetrated into what is now Wisconsin and Minnesota; one of their major goals was to find new sources for furs. Not only did they find an abundance of fur bearing animals and Indians willing to hunt and trap them, but they were pleased to learn that these Indians were willing to travel as far north as Hudson's Bay to exchange their pelts for trade goods.

In the 1700s, independent traders, mostly French, followed the St. Lawrence River to the Great Lakes and then the Minnesota-Ontario boundary waters into the interior. No longer did the Indians have to travel north to Hudson's Bay. Eventually, these traders organized themselves into the Northwest Company and built forts and trading posts from Grand Portage on Lake Superior as far west as Lake Athabasca. In the late 1700s, the Hudson's Bay Company was forced to work south and established competing posts, even reaching into what is now Minnesota, Wisconsin and Michigan. They also moved into the area south of the present U.S.-Canadian border in what are now the western states. Competition between the two companies became intense, even to the point of bloodshed. The rivalry proved very expensive to both companies and a merger was finally negotiated in 1821 under the name of the Hudson's Bay Company.

In the early years, before the merger, the H.B.C. serviced their posts with Scottish immigrants who rowed their long Yorkboats between the headquarters forts on Hudson's Bay and the posts to the south. The

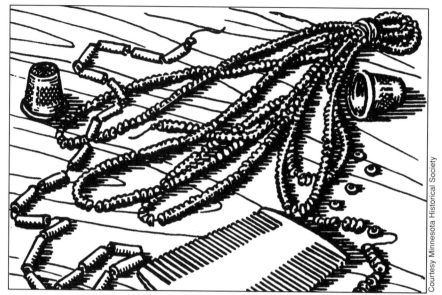

Trinkets for trading

Northwest Company used voyageurs, mostly French Canadian, and their birch canoes to carry trade goods out of Montreal each spring to the posts in the west. They returned in the fall with their loads of furs, taken from animals trapped the previous winter. Because it was impossible to travel to the posts in the far west and return in a single season, other voyageurs who wintered at trading posts in the west (including Minnesota, the Dakotas, Ontario, Manitoba and Saskatchewan) brought furs to Grand Portage on Lake Superior. There they rendezvoused each July with the voyageurs from Montreal and exchanged their furs for trade goods, including such items as kettles, blankets, firearms, ball and powder, tobacco, knives, clothing, beads, combs, cloth, sewing instruments, flour, salt, liquors, etc.

The American Fur Company came on the scene in this part of the continent in the early 1800s. Because no one was absolutely certain where the U.S.-Canadian border was located, they operated for awhile in both countries. When the boundary was finally surveyed and established in 1821 (except for the Northwest Angle of the Lake of the Woods), the newly merged Hudson's Bay Company withdrew to the north and the American Fur Company retreated to posts south of the border. They still competed, however, by trying to entice the Indians to cross the border. The Americans were at a disadvantage since the U.S. Government would not allow them to trade liquor for furs. The A.F.C. shipped its pelts to St. Louis and in later years to the Twin Cities and from there east.

The Columbia Fur Company was also American and it operated several posts on the Upper Mississippi and its watershed.

During the first 200 years of fur trading on this part of the continent, scores of trading posts and forts were constructed on the rivers and connecting lakes. Many were only for a winter season; others were more permanent and serviced the surrounding area for many years. Although we know the general location of most of them through the journals of explorers and traders and through oral histories, we know the exact location of relatively few.

The Gull Lake Region was a prime area for taking furs of all kinds: beaver,

Tools and cooking utensils for trading

mink, marten, fisher, lynx, bobcat, muskrat, weasel, fox, bear, wolf, etc. It is somewhat surprising, therefore, that the historic records of Minnesota Trading Posts say so little about the post on Gull Lake. We know it was located between Round and Gull near the St. Columba Mission. It was called the Lynde Trading post. It is assumed that was the name of the founder, but we know nothing about when it was started or how long it was in existence. The building, at least, was still there in 1867 when the Ojibwe were moved to White Earth. Whether or not business was transacted there up until that time, we don't know. There are also occasional references to a Round Lake Trading post.

There were other nearby trading posts, easily accessed in one day from Gull Lake. They were at the following locations:

confluence of the Crow Wing and the Mississippi (became the Village of Crow Wing),

Crow Island — also at the mouth of the Crow Wing,

Crow Wing village in 1859 as pictured in Harpers magazine

mouth of the Partridge River (where it enters the Crow Wing),

Leaf River — possibly where it enters the Crow Wing,

Pine River and

Whitefish Lake (2 posts).

The post at the mouth of the Crow Wing was one of the most important in what is now Minnesota. It was both large and permanent. Villages of whites and Indians sprang up there; it died shortly after the founding of Brainerd. The post was operated by a number of independent traders in the 1800's, including Perrault, McGill, Rice, Aitkin and Beaulieu. There are some estimates that the population at its peak may have exceeded 600.

Both Hole-in-the-Days resided there from time to time and the Ojibwe who lived on or near the site were considered part of the Gull Lake Pillager Tribe and were under the jurisdiction of the Hole-in-the-Days.

The first road in Minnesota was built between Fort Snelling and Fort Ripley — and then on to the village of Crow Wing.

Beaulieu's house was moved to Brainerd, along with several other houses from the village of Crow Wing. It was identified in 1996 and has now been restored and returned to the original historic location.

Most trading posts in the central lakes area were built in the early 1800's, but there were forts, which also served as trading posts, built much earlier by the French in what is now Minnesota:

1679 — Duluth at Grand Portage on Lake Superior,

1686 – Perrot on Lake Pepin – Fort St. Antoine,

1695 – Le Sueur on the Mississippi on Prairie Island – Fort Isle Pel'e,

1699 – Le Sueur on the Mankato River (Blue Earth) – Fort L'Hullier and

1732 – Pierre La Verendrye on the Lake of the Woods – Fort St. Charles, Northwest Angle

We also know that Louis La Verendrye was trading on the Mississippi in the Leech Lake area in 1753.

When Zebulon Pike traveled up the Mississippi in 1805-06, he found several trading posts in operation on Leech and Sandy Lakes.

As stated earlier, the Ojibwe traders first brought to this region by Duluth probably called on the Sioux when they lived on Gull Lake.

The legendary voyageurs who followed Duluth's explorations in 1679 and transported trade goods to the Indians and furs back to Montreal very likely also visited Gull Lake. Although most of the voyageur operations were north of the present U.S.-Canadian border, some of them worked their way south and west of present day Duluth – starting with the St. Louis River and the Savanna Portage.

Gull Lake Under Three Flags

Irrespective of Native American ownership, Gull Lake was part of ter ritory claimed by France from 1671 to 1762 and again from 1800 to 1803. In between it was claimed by Spain. The lake was part of the Louisiana Purchase in 1803 and thus became a part of the United States.

Before Minnesota became a state (1858) it was a part of several different territories, in this order: Louisiana, Missouri, Unorganized, Michigan, Wisconsin, Iowa, Unorganized and Minnesota.

In Summary

The prehistoric generations of American Indians who lived on Gull Lake found all they needed for survival: wild rice, maple sap, berries, nuts, fish, big and small game, animal hides for clothing, hides and bark for housing, clay for pots and materials such as stone and wood from which to fashion tools and weapons. Although the coming of the Europeans brought many problems for the Native Americans, it did provide opportunities to make life a little easier and more enjoyable. Whiteman wanted the Indians' furs and for them he would trade guns, powder, shot, knives, axes, pots, kettles, combs, needles, cloth, jewelry, etc.

CHAPTER VI
Logging

From the time of the arrival of the early fur traders on the Mississippi river and its tributaries in the late 1700s to the middle of the next century, the fur industry supported the entire economy of the area we now call Minnesota, but from the mid-1800s to the early 1900s, logging was clearly dominant.

In 1837, the United States government entered into a treaty[1] with Minnesota Indian tribes which included the purchase of the triangle of land formed by the St. Croix and the Mississippi Rivers. The base of the inverted triangle was the north shore of Mille Lacs Lake. This area was then made available to white settlers and loggers. Although there were hardwood forests in the triangle, it was the white and red pines the lumbermen were after. Early settlers reported the pines were so tall and thick that trails were often so dark in daytime it was almost like evening. Others said that it was difficult to read a newspaper in the heart of the forest.

It was here, in this triangle, that logging had its beginning as an industry in the area we now know as Minnesota. It began in the Stillwater area in the late 1830s and spread north until it reached Mille Lacs Lake in the 1880s. Logging began on the Crow Wing River in 1847, making it one of the first regions to be harvested.

The lumberjacks of the north country have given us a heritage nearly as romantic and legendary as that of the voyageurs. The stories of Paul Bunyan are, of course, delightful in their exaggeration; nevertheless, the logger was in his own way a genuine hero of the north woods. He provided the lumber with which we built our nation. A rapidly growing United States needed schools and homes and churches and shops and industrial buildings; the forests of North America seemed to contain an endless source of oak, pine, birch, maple, cedar, and spruce with which to do the job.

Cities such as St. Paul, Minneapolis, Omaha, Des Moines, Kansas City and Topeka were built almost entirely of Minnesota lumber.

It is tempting for us, in retrospect, to think of the lumberjack as a villain who denuded the landscape and exposed the earth to erosion.

But before we treat him too harshly we must realize—

- The lumber was essential to the building of the new country,
- That the people of that day viewed the supply as endless,
- That it was common to work a ten-hour day and a six-day week with no vacations and only an occasional holiday; and little thought was given, therefore, to the recreational value of the forests,
- That land had to be cleared to plant crops to feed a new, industrialized society and
- That it was assumed the forests would grow back—and they did (although in many areas we traded the noble pines for scrub oak and popple).

True, management could have planned better; it was not necessary to rape the beautiful shorelines of lakes and rivers, and more thought should have been given to the future. But all that is now history; and because of the circumstances of that time, which we have just cited, we must not judge the logger of another generation by the standards of today. The lumberjack was only doing his job and doing it well.

The logging camp was a unique community out of our nation's past, a chapter in our history well worth remembering. The lumberjack worked in a remarkable setting. Besides the beauty of the rivers and lakes, there was an abundance of wildlife. In addition to the animals and birds found in the region today, the last of the elk and caribou were still to be seen. In the early years of logging history the Indians still lived much as they had for generations and the lumberjack was privileged to see their lodges and birchbark canoes.

All logging camps were not alike—but just about. For a contingent of from one hundred to a hundred and fifty men there were usually three bunkhouses, a cooking shack, an office and supply headquarters, a shelter for the horses, a blacksmith shop and forge, a shanty where saws were sharpened, and a root cellar for storing vegetables. Construction was usually of rough pine (mainly red) and meant to be temporary. When an area was logged out, only the windows, doors, frames and hardware were salvaged and moved to the new location. Two or three years was the average life of a logging camp.

The bunkhouses were long and narrow with double-deck beds lining both walls. Tradition has it that Pullman designed his railroad sleeping cars after visiting a logging camp bunkhouse. Winters were often bitter cold and the only source of heat was a potbellied stove stationed in the aisle between the bunks. Insulation was not used and it was not unusual for a logger to awaken in the morning with his hair frozen to the frost-covered wall! Lines were strung near the ceiling for drying clothes, perhaps more wet with sweat than moisture from the snow. No doubt the aroma added to the atmosphere! And yet, it is said the teamsters were housed separately near the horse barn because they smelled like their animals. On very cold days, the lumberjacks were inclined to wear more than one suit of long underwear and it was customary on those occasions to wear the clean suit next to the skin and pull on the used suit over the other. Lice were a problem in many logging camps and were sometimes so bad the men gave up fighting them and just learned to live with them.

The lumberjacks were of mixed heritage. The early loggers came from as far east as New England and fresh out of the Michigan and Wisconsin woods. A U.S. Senator from the state of Maine, for example, expressed his anxiety over losing his state's best young men to the Midwest. But "locals" soon joined the crews and made for a real melting pot of all nationalities. Most were first generation North Americans providing an interesting mixture of brogues and accents.

By testimony of old lumberjacks, life in the logging camps was nowhere as boisterous as portrayed in movies or legend. Spending all of the daylight hours at hard work, six days a week, left little energy for rowdyism. Furthermore, alcohol was strictly forbidden in most camps. In fact, alcoholics were known to "take the cure" by going to work in the woods. Although many smoked, chewing was more common; the men needed both hands free in their work. Card playing was a favorite evening pastime; dry beans often substituted for poker chips. Sunday meant wash day (usually outside) and relaxation.

In this harsh environment, mealtime was really something to look forward to; the lumberjacks enjoyed excellent food and plenty of it. Meat was served at every meal and included ham, fresh beef and veal, bologna, wieners, salt pork, pork sausage, bacon and liver. Fish and wild game added still more variety.

Vegetables were limited to those which could be stored in root cellars such as beans, potatoes, cabbage, carrots, rutabagas, onions and parsnips. Beans were prepared in iron kettles or baked in the oven.

Breads, cakes, doughnuts, and pies were baked fresh daily.

While breakfast and supper were served in the camp, the noon meal was often brought out to the men by sleigh or "swingdingle." Although the food was usually more than adequate, the table setting was austere, with tin plates and cups and metal utensils (steel, but not stainless). Traditionally, meals were eaten in silence, to save time and to preserve the peace.

A welcome break in camp routine was the occasional visit of a circuit rider preacher or "sky pilot." Some became legends in their own right.

Treaties between Minnesota Indian Tribes and the United States Government,* many of which opened the area to logging.

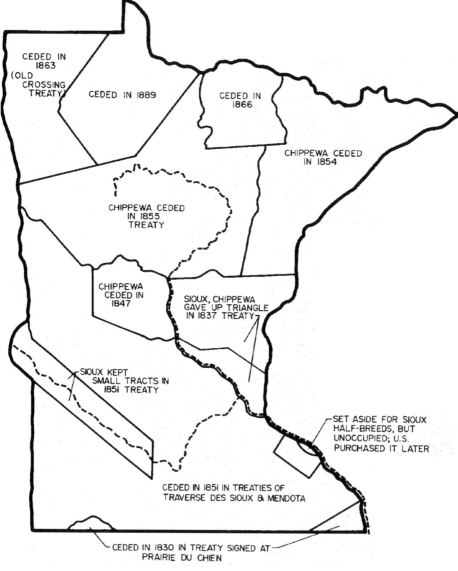

CEDED IN 1863 (OLD CROSSING TREATY)

CEDED IN 1889

CEDED IN 1866

CHIPPEWA CEDED IN 1854

CHIPPEWA CEDED IN 1855 TREATY

CHIPPEWA CEDED IN 1847

SIOUX, CHIPPEWA GAVE UP TRIANGLE IN 1837 TREATY

SIOUX KEPT SMALL TRACTS IN 1851 TREATY

SET ASIDE FOR SIOUX HALF-BREEDS, BUT UNOCCUPIED; U.S. PURCHASED IT LATER

CEDED IN 1851 IN TREATIES OF TRAVERSE DES SIOUX & MENDOTA

CEDED IN 1830 IN TREATY SIGNED AT PRAIRIE DU CHIEN

Courtesy Minnesota Historical Society

*Red Lake Reserve not shown because that tribe never did sign a treaty.

Most loggers were family men who looked at their job as just another way of making a living and supported a wife and kids living farther south, where they would return come spring. Although some men stayed on for the drives down rivers and across lakes, logging was mostly a winter occupation. Swamps and hoards of flies and mosquitoes were too much to cope with in summer. Besides, it was much easier to skid the heavy logs over snow than across bare ground. After spring break-up, the teamsters took their horses and oxen and headed south to work on roads and farms. Many loggers were farmers.

Lest we leave the impression lumberjacks were without sin, let us hasten to add that most made up for their regulated camp life when they hit town on holidays or at the end of the logging season. Frontier towns were crowded with saloons and brothel houses, and many a man blew his stake in a matter of hours. The village of Walker reportedly had 40 saloons.

It was the Upper Mississippi and its tributaries that brought the logs to the sawmills where they were converted into lumber. The last significant log drive on the Mississippi was in 1919.

During the last decade of the 1800s railroad tracks were laid throughout the northern part of Minnesota, facilitating the hauling of logs to the mills. Although the mainlines were standard width, many of the tracks into the logging camps were narrow gauge. Other steam-operated equipment became available around the turn of the century, including power shovels, power cranes, and locomotives that moved on caterpillar trends instead of wheels on tracks. These caterpillar type tracks, on which most of the heavy equipment moved, are said to have led to the development of the military tanks used in World War I and subsequent wars.

Logging camps had a unique culture and language; here is some loggers' jargon:

stove lids – pancakes
java or black jack – coffee
cow – milk
cackle berries or hens' fruit – eggs
gravel – salt
Mexican gravel – pepper
sand – sugar
whistle berries or firecrackers – beans
mulligan – stew
Adam's or Eve's fruit – apples
grub – food
sow belly – salt pork
red horse – roast pork
dingle – a pantry or storeroom off the kitchen

swingdingle – a sleigh that brought food out to the lumberjacks in the woods

timber cruisers – men who looked for good stands of timber to be cut

scalers – men who measured the logs that had been cut

river pigs — lumberjacks who kept logs moving down rivers

peaveys or pike poles – used to break-up log jams on rivers

deadheads – logs that absorbed water and sank; sometimes one end would float

cookies – cooks; the headcook was called the "bull Cook"

deacon's seat – benches in front of bunks where the jacks socialized

wood butcher – carpenter

smithy – blacksmith

camp dentist – sharpened axes and the teeth of saws

As we have mentioned earlier, logging began in Minnesota in 1839, following the Treaty of 1837, in the triangle of land formed by the Mississippi and St. Croix Rivers. The first mills were in the Stillwater area. By 1880, operations had moved north in this inverted triangle of land to Mille Lacs Lake.

Meanwhile, other logging operations were begun at St. Anthony (now Minneapolis) in 1848 and a sawmill was established in Winona in 1852.

The Crow Wing watershed had an abundance of white pine; in fact, the Ojibwe called it the Pine River. An agreement was reached with Chief Hole-in-the-Day I in 1847 to permit logging in that area. The treaty gave him a stipend of $1,000 a year. The payment later went to his son. In the first winter (1847-48), a million and a half feet of longs were harvested; they were sent down stream that spring.

When the Crow Wing area had been logged off, visitors reported that all they could see was acres of huge, waist-high, sawed-off, white pine stumps.

Many names are associated with the logging of the Crow Wing watershed (including Gull Lake and Gull River), but none remain as familiar to us as that of Frederick Weyerhaueser, German born lumber baron. Founded in Illinois in 1860, his company moved its influence steadily northward and included this area when it purchased the Pine Tree Company of Little Falls and then, in cooperation with other lumber groups, purchased huge land holdings from the Northern Pacific Railroad. Today the Weyerhaueser enterprises extend to the west coast.

There was much cooperation, and sometimes collusion, among the lumber magnates. Sometimes legal partnerships were organized; other times there were negotiations behind the scenes, such as in the bidding on timber on Indian lands.

Many names are remembered from these years, including Walker, Backus, Akeley, Shevlin, Pillsbury[2] and others. Some operators were not so big but are remembered because they gave their names to communities or townships or other landmarks. King Staples, for example, logged the area where a city now bears his name from 1878 to 1881. In later years the Dower Lumber Company operated in the same region and a little lake west of Staples is called Dower Lake to this day.

The Wilson Brothers, George and William, of Park Rapids, were among the names associated with the logging of the Crow Wing and its tributaries. They are good examples of "middle management" of that day. They often worked for, or were financed by, the lumber magnates and, in turn, actually planned the cutting and hired the men. In George Wilson's memoirs, as recorded by Charles Vandersluis of Bemidji, he tells of:

John Moberg operating on the Shell River in the 1880s;

The Wilson brothers supervising the cutting and sending of forty or fifty million feet of logs down the river in 1893 from the sixth, seventh, and eighth Crow Wing Lakes—they were all marked for Akeley and sent to his Minneapolis mill;

Jerry Howe's operation on the Eighth Crow Wing Lake in 1898, with all logs being sold in Minneapolis;

The construction of the Walker-Akeley mill on the Upper Crow Wing in 1898;

The Wilson's operation on Eighth Crow Wing during the winters of 1899 to 1901 where they built a dam at the outlet; and

The operations of Carpenter and Lamb in 1905.

Once the logs reached the Mississippi, they were usually handled by the Mississippi and Rum River Company on their way to Minneapolis or dropped off at mills along the way. Logs were all registered to their owners in the Surveyor General's office; they were branded much as cattle (a special mallet was used with a design in the head).

H.B. Morrison had a sawmill operation at Motley from the 1800s into this century, making that community one of the busiest lumbering centers of that day. Morrison also manufactured bricks.

Wanigans (floating kitchens) were used on all of the Crow Wing Lakes and on the river as well. In high water, paddlewheeled steamboats ventured up both the Crow Wing and the Long Prairie Rivers but were often stuck on sandbars. The "Lotta Lee" was marooned on a bar on its maiden voyage up the Crow Wing and there perished when the ice went out the next spring. After the railroad came to Motley, grain was hauled from Long Prairie down the river on barges to that community.

The lumberjacks of old were a singing people, and during the peak years the industry was glamorized by a number of ballads, including "The Crow Wing Drive":

Says White Pine Tom to Arkansaw
"There's one more drive that I'd like to strike."
Says Arkansaw, "What can it be?"
"It's the Crow Wing River for the Old Pine Tree."

Gull River and the Brainerd Area

The Gull River, which flows into the Crow Wing, became the access to another huge area for logging. Since it is so close to Brainerd, it is not surprising that the same developers logged the forests up the Mississippi from that town. What they couldn't reach by water, they harvested by rail by the end of the century.

As in most parts of Minnesota, a conglomerate of lumbermen opened the country and harvested the timber. Pillsbury, Chase, Leavitt and Horn, all of Minneapolis, were the principal owners of the forests.

Once the trees adjacent to the waters of the Gull chain of lakes had been harvested, it became necessary to build railroads. In 1889, a short lived narrow gauge railroad was constructed north and west of Gull Lake under the corporate name of "Gull Lake and Northern Railroad Co,"[3] with Charles Pillsbury as president. The logs it carried were dumped into Lake Margaret and herded in rafts, by steamboat, across Gull Lake and then down river to the waiting sawmills of the Gull River Lumber Company. Highways 13 and 77 are partially built on old railroad grades.

Stuart Mills, Sr., long time Brainerd Oldsmobile dealer and a founder of the Mills Fleet Farm Stores, as a young man piloted the last steamboat (a paddle wheeler) on the lake to push and pull these rafts of logs across Gull Lake to the river outlet. He also operated a ferry service between the railroad terminal and the west end of the lake.

The Gull River Lumber Company mills were located near the place where the Burlington Northern and Santa Fe crosses Gull River on the route between Brainerd and Staples. Here, in 1880, the village of Gull River became the first incorporated community in Cass County. Brainerd (called "New Town" by the Indians) had been platted in 1871. At their peak, the Gull River Mills employed 150 men and the community included more than twenty houses, an office building, boarding houses, a store, postoffice and a depot. The total population reached about 400 at its peak. Some believe the house on the north side of highway 210 where it crosses the Gull River was part of the village.

The company offices were located on the east bank of the Gull River, while the mill itself was on the west bank.

The Gull River Lumber Company lasted only 12 years; that is all the time it took to deplete the Gull watershed of its mighty forests. The company boasted that it could turnout 80,000 feet of lumber in a ten hour work day and shipped more than 200 railroad carloads of lumber a month.

In the early 1900's rafts of logs continued to cross Gull Lake and go down stream, but it was a mere trickle compared to the latter years of the previous century. With the construction of a dam on the Gull River in 1911, it was all over.

Gradually, logging operations moved farther north, reaching the Leech

The Gull River Lumber Mill and crew.

A sketch showing another view of the Gull River Lumber Company.

Lake area in the 1890's. Once the navigable portions of the Mississippi had been logged off, it became necessary to construct railroads to reach the in land areas there as well.

Brainerd, Walker and Bemidji were connected by the Brainerd and Northern Minnesota Railroad. It reached Walker in 1896 and was extended to Bemidji in 1897-99. In 1901 it was purchased by the Minnesota and International Railway – with offices in Brainerd.

Park Rapids and Cass lake were connected by the Park Rapids and Leech Lake Railway in 1899. This line was purchased by the Great Northern in 1907.

Federal Dam, Cass Lake, Bemidji and Plummer were connected in 1909 with an extension (east to west) of the Canadian based Minneapolis, St. Paul and Sault St. Marie Railroad (Soo Line).

The Great Northern also crossed this area from east to west through the village of Cass Lake.

All existing railroads in the area are now a part of the Burlington Northern-Santa Fe system.

With the passing of a century and the coming of a second growth of trees, logging has been revived as a major industry, and it is once again contributing to the economy of the Gull Lake area. Gone are the logging camps and the old crosscut saws. Today, logs are hauled by truck and harvested by chainsaws and sophisticated machinery. Lumberjacks are now called "loggers" and they spend their nights in their own homes with their families.

A typical narrow gauge logging railroad.

A log corduroy road – usually used in swampy areas.

Spring comes to a turn-of-the-century logging camp.

A swingdingle, used for delivering lunch to loggers.

Some logging trains did not run on tracks.

A turn-of-the-century logging train.

Loggers huddle around a barrel stove. Note the clothes drying from the ceiling.

A logging camp dining room.

Footnotes

[1]This is the same treaty on which present day Ojibwe base their claim to hunt and fish Mille Lacs and other lakes to the east at will.

[2]The Pillsbury State Forest on the southwest side of Gull Lake includes land provided by the Pillsbury family. This is the same family that milled flour and expanded into a variety of enterprises. The company is now owned by a British corporation.

[3]It was also called the "Spider Lake Line" and the "Minnesota Logging Railroad."

CHAPTER VII
The Lake Becomes a Center for Recreation

During the logging era, buildings began to appear on the Gull Lake chain of lakes. Most were nothing more than cabins or shacks, but a few were year around homes. Among the first of the white pioneer families to live on the lake was that of Casper Mills. His sons, Stewart and Henry, later became successful car dealers in Brainerd. Stewart sold Oldsmobiles while Henry chose Fords. After World War II they purchased and developed the system of Mills Fleet Farm Stores. Stewart later bought out Henry. Stu's twin sons, also named Stewart and Henry, along with their mother, Helen, took over the business after their father's death. They also re-established Mills Motor (Ford) in Baxter. The dealership now also includes General Motors cars.

As mentioned in Chapter VI, it was Stewart Mills Sr. who in the final years of logging towed rafts across the lake to Gull River using a paddle-boat steamer. Mills also operated gasoline-powered launches, providing both freight and passenger service to all parts of the chain of lakes. He connected with the trains at Nisswa and later with the road (then more of a trail) from Brainerd to Walker where it passed between Round and Gull Lakes. His operation was originally called the Gull Lake Boat Livery; it was later named the Nisswa Boat Livery. Another boat was operated by S.V. Long after Mills moved on.

The Mills boat service made it possible for hunting and fishing camps to spring up on the chain of lakes; Casper operated one of the first.

On the west side of Gull Lake a small cluster of cabins became known as Portview.

A logging camp was located along the beach northwest from Sandy Point. This had been the site of an Indian village.

Several buildings appeared on the north end of the lake on and near the Gull Lake-Round Lake Narrows, where there had been so much American Indian activity down through history. This, of course, was also the site of the St. Columba Mission and a trading post. In 1860 there were eight homes of whites in that vicinity.

Stewart Mills Sr., on the deck of his launch. His passengers are probably arriving at or leaving Anderson's Rocky Point Resort.

In 1869, the Reuben Gray family built a home on the north side of the creek that runs between the lakes, and the stream was originally known to whites as *Gray's Creek*. John Bishop established an inn, or halfway house, on the south side of the creek and eventually, the stream came to be called *Bishops's Creek*. Shortly thereafter Web Hill built an inn on an old logging camp site three miles farther north on Nisswa Lake, which was then known as *Three Mile Lake* – so he called his place "Three Mile Ranch." The three miles refers to the distance from Bishop's inn on the thoroughfare. Both places were on an old trail to Leech Lake which ran from Brainerd to Hackensack and then to Onigum and Walker. The trail was originally used by Indians; later it was improved for use by horse-drawn vehicles and bicycles. Still later, with the invention of the automobile, it became a driveable road, the predecessor to Highway 371. It is believed the very first summer cabin was built by Ira White in 1878 on Hole-in-the-Day Bay.[1]

A post office was opened at the thoroughfare in 1885 with the name *Gladstone*. It closed the next year. The post office was moved to *Smiley*, which later was to become known as *Nisswa*. Leon Lum, a Brainerd attorney of whom we will speak more, later, along with some friends, turned the abandoned post office building into a club house. In 1901, it was incorporated as the *Gull Lake Outing Club*. It was also called "the Gull Lake Hotel" but was basically a private facility.

Lum built a cabin for himself on Nisswa Lake. Other cabins appeared on Nisswa (still called Three Mile lake), including the E.B. Merrill family and the La Moure family, both neighbors of Casper Mills.

Charles White built a cabin between Gull and Ruth Lakes just before the turn of the century.

William "Buff" McNaughton operated a lunch counter and rented fishing boats at the source of the Gull River (east side) starting in 1910. A few years later he moved to Pike Bay. When he died, his uncle John took over and called his operation *Cast a Bait Resort*.

In 1913, a small band of visionary men purchased the area where the St. Columba Mission once stood and plotted it into lots for summer homes. They were J.M Elder, W.A. Barrows (for whom the now extinct mining village south of Brainerd was named), Carl Zapffe (father of the Carl Zapffe who has authored "The Man Who Lived in Three Centuries" and other books) and an author himself of a history of Brainerd and D.L. Fairchild (a mining engineer from Duluth). Actually, all members of the group had a common interest in mining. They called the development "St. Columbo."

The first true resorts on the Gull Lake Chain were both started in the year

The Gull Lake Outing Club, originally the Gladstone Post Office, located at the Gull-Round thoroughfare.

Courtesy Cass County Historical Society

1912; one had the unlikely name of *Ozonite Park*. It was founded by a physician, Dr. John Bemis, and his wife. They fell in love with the area and the doctor closed his St. Paul practice. They proceeded to build a series of housekeeping cabins between Gull and Upper Gull. Later, they built a rather large log lodge where meals were served. They named the lodge "Dreamwold." They had an adopted son, Perce, who eventually took over the operation. It became known as a "Gentiles only resort"; a rather sad commentary on those times.

Hawkinson's *Camp Comfort* was built up the shore from Ozonite Park.

Rocky Point was the setting for the other early resort. It was started by Charles Anderson and his wife, also in 1912, and continued under their sons, Erv, Art and Herb. The original Anderson homestead was built in 1895 and was also on the lake. They relocated on Rocky Point in 1911. Charles also fished the lake commercially.

In later years, Erv built his own resort next door (west) and called it *Dellwood*. Again, it was the Stewart Mills boat service that made it possible for the resorts to operate in the early years. Herb Anderson eventually took over management of the Rocky Point Resort. We will hear more about the Anderson brothers when we talk about Bar Harbor.

Courtesy Carl Zapffe

The Charles and Hannah Anderson family with sons, Art, Erv and Herb and daughter, May

Having mentioned that Anderson was a commercial fisherman, we should add that most large Brainerd area lakes were fished commercially almost up to World War I. Anderson was not the only commercial fisherman on the Gull Lake chain. Even after World War I, the author's father and his friends traded northern pike speared in Gull Lake in winter for groceries at Brainerd stores.

Ducks were also hunted commercially on Gull and other area lakes – such as Mille Lacs. Although most ducks were shot with traditional shotguns over decoys, four gauge shotguns were sometimes bolted to boat decks and used to attack rafts of diving ducks. Most birds were marketed in the big cities along the east coast of the continent.

Grand View Lodge – one of the Grandest of them All!

Grand View Lodge had its origins on the homestead of the William Bergh family. Part of their home was a sort-of factory where wire was manufactured. The property was sold – or almost sold – several times in 1913 and 1914. In 1915, Henry Spalding, a retired sheriff, acquired the site and began to transform it into a hunting and fishing camp. Just one year later his health gave out and, with great reluctance, he sold the property to Marvin Baker and Harry Seaton who had tried to buy it earlier. In 1916, the partners named the place "Grand View Lodge". They immediately had the property surveyed and subdivided into 240 lots, which they originally intended to sell. Shortly thereafter, however, Baker bought out Seaton and went on to develop what eventually became one of the truly great resorts and Conference centers of the Midwest.

Baker was more of a Realtor than a resorter and legend has it that he opened the lodge to give his "cantankerous" wife something to do and to keep her out of his hair!

R.F.B. "Brownie" Cote (the initials stand for Reynolds Frederick Brownlee) purchased the Grand View Lodge in 1937. Both individuals, Cote and Baker, were known as good businessmen and tough negotiators and those who knew them well said they would like to have been present during negotiations! For example, as part of the deal, Baker was allowed to keep the cabin he lived in without charge until he died – and he did – at age 94. Cote, along with partners Fred Rogers and Charles Everett, operated Camp Lincoln for Boys and Camp Lake Hubert for Girls – both on nearby Lake Hubert. Cote purchased

Judy and "Brownie" Cote

Grand View because the parents of the campers did not have a decent place to stay when they dropped their children off, picked them up or visited them. Brownie Cote and his partners in the camp operations had been counselors at the boys camp – then called Blake Camp. The camp was owned by Mr. Blake of Blake School and combined tutoring with an outdoor experience. The young men purchased the boys camp from Mr. Blake in 1927. They then started Camp Lake Hubert for Girls and this was run by Fred Roger's father and mother. Both camps became well known nationally and the sons and daughters of the rich and famous came here for a camping experience.

Cote expanded Grand View greatly and it became one of the first conference centers in rural Minnesota. Today, Grand View may actually be best known for its golf courses, The Pines and The Preserve. The Pines has been rated the number one golf course in Minnesota and named consistently among the top fifty nationally.

Cote also had two operations near Tucson, Arizona: The Desert Willow Guest Ranch and the Tanque Verde Guest Ranch.

Fred Boos, Brownie's son-in-law, took over management of Grand View in 1969 after working under Bob Hartman who had been general manager the previous seven years. Mark Ronnei became general manager in 1988; since that time Fred has concentrated on the golf end of the business. Grand View is also known for it tennis complex. It was the first Minnesota resort to get into tennis in a big way. The impressive array of courts was developed in 1980 and has been rated number one in Minnesota and among the top fifty nationally. A pro is on staff.

The resort prides itself in paying special attention to children. Better Homes and Gardens magazine has rated Grand View among the top seven programs for children in the country. The Cote Foundation helps support free golf and tennis lessons for kids and also helps support a highly suc-

The original Grand View Lodge – no longer in existence.

cessful and innovative reading program for elementary students in the Brainerd-Gull Lake area.

Grand View's main lodge is on the Register of Historic Places of the US Department of Interior. A couple of historic sidelights are worth mentioning. As you walk into the main dining room of the lodge and if you test the floor in front of the maitre d's rostrum, you may detect a trapdoor under the carpet. During the slot machine era of the 1930's and 40's, this is where they hid the machines when they received word that the sheriff was coming!

Speaking of gambling, Governor Luther Youngdahl was staying at Grand View early in his first term of office when he discovered (while on a walk with his sons) the gambling complexes at Bar Harbor and Deauville. At that time gambling was illegal in Minnesota. Although Youngdahl was probably aware of the slot machines in the state he was shocked by the extent of gambling in these two casinos. He returned to the capitol where he strictly enforced the state's no gambling laws from then on.

Paul Newman, the actor, has been a frequent guest at the lodge while racing at the Brainerd International Raceway. The lady guests have especially enjoyed his visits!

Speaking of crime, John Dillinger, the notorious outlaw and bank robber of the 1930's, once stayed at a little resort called Luann's Cottages just to the right of Grand View as you face the lake. He of course registered under an assumed name. The owners remembered him as a pleasant and kindly man who taught children how to shoot at targets. One day the resort owner picked up the mail in Nisswa along with a telegram to the outlaw which simply said, "Grandma is coming." Dillinger left immediately. It turned out "Grandma" was a code word for the FBI. It is rumored that lesser hoods stayed at Breezy Point.

Today, Grand View Lodge hosts many family reunions, golf groups, honeymooners and families from around the country. They come to enjoy the beautiful beach, deluxe accommodations and fine restaurants, serving some of the best food in the region. In 1999 Grand View became a year-round operation.

Nisswa

The community of Nisswa was originally called *Smiley*. It was named for the Ernest Smiley family who first settled here and later plotted their homestead into lots, which they called "Smiley's Subdivision." The township was also called Smiley.

Leon Lum, the Brainerd attorney we mentioned earlier, became interested in the community when he and some friends built a cabin on Lake Hubert. Lum next built a cabin on Nisswa Lake and was a leader in forming the Gull Lake Outing Club on the Gull — Round thoroughfare. He was instrumental in changing the name of the community and its post office to Nisswa in 1908. The railroad station was renamed Nisswa the following year. The name was derived from the Ojibwe word for "three" — nisswe. The significance of the name lies in the fact that Nisswa Lake was then called Three Mile Lake and Web Hill had called the half-way house Three Mile Ranch, as mentioned earlier, both were approximately three miles north of Bishop's Inn on the Gull-Round thoroughfare.

Leon E. Lum, Brainerd attorney and Gull Lake area pioneer. He gave Nisswa its name. He donated a large piece of land on Rice Lake, an overflow of the Mississippi, to the city of Brainerd; it was named "Lum Park" in appreciation.

Three Mile Lake had been called *Middle Fishtrap* by early whites before Hill built his ranch. Upper and Lower Fishtrap Lakes are now known as *Clark* and *Roy Lakes* respectively.

Margaret Lake was named for Margaret Cobbin; she and her husband owned considerable land on the lake. Previously the lake had been called *Gilpatrick* – named for a lumber camp cook who, along with his horses, fell through the ice and drowned.

Nisswa was a natural location for a community. It was not only located on the Gull chain of Lakes, but was also on the railroad and the Leech Lake trail – which became Highway 19 and later Highway 371. Automobiles started using the road in 1917.

The railroad originally crossed the Mississippi at northeast Brainerd (later at Baxter) and ran north from there to the Lake Hubert station. From here it continued north to Nisswa, Pequot Lakes (originally called Sibley), Jenkins, Pine River, Mildred, Backus, the ghost towns of Lothrop and Cypher, and finally reached Walker in 1896. From there it went to Bemidji and eventually to International Falls. Known first as the Brainerd and Northern Minnesota Railroad, it was purchased by the Minnesota and International Railroad. The Northern Pacific eventually came to operate the railroad and took ownership in 1942. No longer in operation, much of the right-of-way is part of the Paul Bunyan Trail.

During the 1930's, the *Spotlight* nightclub was located in Nisswa and with its big bands and gambling made the community known state-wide. Nisswa in those days was perceived quite differently by different people. Some thought of it as a focal point for fun and revelry; others probably agreed with the evangelist who said, while holding meetings in Brainerd, "I'd like to put a banner across the main street that would say, Welcome to Nisswa – gateway to Hell!"

Today Nisswa is a thriving tourist center, the city limits have been expanded to include the whole township and its business community provides all kinds of services to tourists and residents of Gull and neighboring lakes.

Before going on, we should say more about Leon Lum, who did so much to develop Nisswa, including the filing of a plat for a townsite by that name in 1921. Lum came to Brainerd from his birthplace in Anoka in 1881 and practiced law on the second floor of the First National Bank Building on the corner of 6th and Front streets. In 1901 he moved his law practice to Duluth, where his brother, Clarence, was a physician. Lum's first love, however, remained the Gull chain of Lakes and he spent a great deal of time there. He died on Nisswa Lake, after shoveling snow, in 1926.

Tourism Comes to the South End of the Lake

Two men from Kansas City also recognized the recreational potential of this magnificent lake – John W. Harrison and Chester T. Start. Together they constructed the first Pine Beach Golf Course on the south end of the lake. The land earlier was part of 10,000 acres purchased by Harrison's father. It was no small undertaking to carve greens and fairways out of a wilderness of pine and birch. Every available farmer who owned a team of horses was hired to help – 100 teams in all! Harrison and Start were the first corporators of Pine Beach Golf, Inc. and Pine Beach, Inc. More money was needed and Arthur Roberts, a nephew of Kahler – the Rochester hotel Magnate- purchased about twenty-five percent of the stock. A number of Brainerd business and professional men also invested. It was then called the Brainerd Pine Beach Hotel Company.

In 1929, the large resort hotel opened on Pine Beach (first called "Brainerd Pine Beach Hotel," then "Robert's Pine Beach Hotel," and now "Madden's Inn"). The timing couldn't have been worse; both men lost large sums of money during the great depression — Start even suffered a nervous breakdown.

Ruttgers on Gull

The Ruttgers name has been closely tied to the resort business in Minnesota for many years. The original Ruttger's resort, on Bay Lake, is among the oldest in the state and is the oldest resort under continuous family ownership and operation (since 1898). As the sons of the founding family spread their wings the name appeared on other Minnesota lakes and may still be found on Lake Bemidji and Sugar Lake near Grand Rapids as well as on Bay Lake. There was also a resort on Whitefish Lake.

Ruttger's on Gull was originally called Pine Beach Lodge; it is now called Pine Portage and is a part of the Madden's enterprises. In 1931, Ruttger's opened as one of the largest resorts in northern Minnesota — 25 cabins and a lodge, American plan. It was the first resort in the state with a bathroom in every cabin!

The resort was opened by Max Ruttger. Up until that time he and his family had been a part of the original Ruttger operation on Bay Lake. In late August, 1930, Max and his older brother (by two years) Alex — and their wives — drove to Pine Beach on Gull Lake and met with Chester Start. Buz Ruttger (Max II) remembers Start as a super-salesman. Start showed the Ruttgers his proposed site for a resort: it was part of the 10,000 acres purchased by Harrison's father. Although a new resort would mean competition, Start had the wisdom to know that the more resorts on that end of the lake the better the business for everyone; it was important to make that area well known in the state as a vacation destination. In fact, just a few years later, Max and Jack Madden encouraged Merrill Cragun to open his resort, featuring housekeeping cabins.

Buz can still remember how excited his father was when they returned to Bay Lake. The deal was consummated and construction was started on September 5, 1930 for an American Plan resort; Max was a man of action!

Ruttger served as his own contractor and hired twenty-five carpenters. On November 15, Buz and his father drove to Gull Lake to release the crew because all twenty-five cabins and the lodge were completed. They all went deer hunting!

The electrical work was done that winter and the plumbers came in the spring. The resort was ready when the tourist season began in the spring of '31.

It was not easy; in 1931 the country was in the depths of the Great

Depression, and then came World War II with gas rationing and the intense defense and war effort. Buz joined the navy as a pilot trainer. The resort remained open, however, and eventually prospered.

In 1947, Max turned the resort over to Buz and his wife, Carol.

The Gull Lake resort was a seasonal business, but the family opened a second resort in Florida, giving them a year-around operation.

Ruttgers sold their Gull Lake operation to Maddens in 1969; it was renamed Pine Portage Resort.

Madden's Resort and Conference Center

Jack Madden opened a soda fountain and a cigar counter on Ruttger's porch in 1931. He owned his own business and paid Ruttger a percentage

Courtesy Jack Madden

Roberts Pine Beach Hotel

"of the take" as rent. Jack's cousin was the "soda jerk" and his uncle, Tom Madden, brought in a slot machine concession.

The next year, 1932, Jack Madden operated the Pine Beach Golf Course for Start and Harrison and their incorporators; he moved his soda fountain and cigar counter there as well. In 1934, Madden purchased the golf course and his brother, Jim, went to work for him at that time. Jim Madden entered the partnership in 1937; the partnership added John Arnold in 1957; he had been Director of Food Services for Northwest Airlines. Maddens were originally from Stillwater; Arnold from Brainerd.

In 1936 Jack Madden and Chester Start built a resort on Mission Point, so named because missionaries came there from St. Columba to try to convert the Indians who lived on the south end of the lake. (The point where St. Columba church was located is also known as Mission Point.)

The housekeeping resort consisted of three cabins, three garages and attached maid quarters.

In 1937, when Jim Madden joined the business, Tom Madden (Jim and Jack's uncle) dropped out.

In 1941, Jack and his wife Peg Madden bought out Chester Start's share of Mission Point. They built cabins for 24 people by using the existing structures and building onto them. The following year Mission Point was re-named "the Lodge." While building up the Lodge, the Madden brothers purchased a Little Falls Hotel (built in 1923 as an Elks Club and Home) and renamed it the Pine Edge Inn. In that same year, they also purchased Madden's first sizable piece of equipment, a Farmall tractor, for $600 for use on the Pine Beach Golf Course.

Jim Madden was drafted for the service in 1942 and Jack and Peg were left to run the Madden Lodge, Golf Course and Pine Edge Inn by themselves.

In 1946, Jim returned from the service and he and Jack remodeled the old Clubhouse into rooms and started a new wing that would house a coffee shop, dining room and kitchen. This wing was completed in 1947 with an additional 20 new rooms. During 1948 and 49, two dining rooms were built called "The Prime Rib Room" and "The Garden Room." Six years later, the building continued with the first 20 rooms of the Voyageur Resort breaking ground, which also included an office and a VIP suite.

In 1959, Lumbertown USA was built, along with a convention facility named Town Hall. During the early 1960's, Madden's opened a Par 3 Social 9 golf course and the O'Madden Pub. In 1964 a devastating fire burned the whole Inn and all its additions. It was the eve of July 4 and the grand opening of the new Pub. Jim Madden considers the highlight of his career being open for business the day after the fire. "It may have been the best thing that has happened to us,' he said, "It was a horrible building. Fires are always a disaster, but we came out of the ashes pretty good."

In the mid-60's, a new Golf Club was built and the partners purchased Robert's Pine Beach Hotel, which they renamed the Madden Inn. They also started work on the 18 hole golf course called "Pine Beach West." The first 9 holes were called "Sylvan." In 1968 the new Clubhouse was opened which featured four apartments and a pool. The partners also purchased Ruttger's Pine Beach Lodge in 1969 and renamed it the Pine Portage Resort. The Green Hill Resort and 80 acres of property were purchased from Lee and Ruth Goetting, former owners of the Robert's Hotel.

The 1970's saw many new additions to the Madden property. In 1970 a new addition to Town Hall was built, along with the Lumber Baron Steak House. During 1973, the second 9 holes of Pine Beach West was opened and in 1975 the course was completed. Other additions in the 70's saw a cookout area and tennis courts.

During the 1980's, croquet lawns were added and in April of 1986, the new Town Hall Conference Center was opened which is among the finest conference facilities in the nation.

A new partner was added in 1989 when C. Brian Thuringer, son-in-law of Jim, came to Madden's Resorts after managing the Pine Edge Inn for 8 years.

Growth has continued with the addition of a new Tennis and Croquet Club, which houses the "starting point" for many of the Madden's recreational activities, along with the Par Fecto Pizza and Sub Shoppe. The Classic golf course and clubhouse were, added making Madden's the largest golf enterprise in the state – with a total of 63 holes!

It has been a long and amazing journey from a cigar counter and soda fountain operation on Max Ruttger's porch to a resort and conference complex serving more than 500 customers daily, the largest in Minnesota!

Craguns and the Paul Bunyan Connection

In 1934, a twin cities' printer copyrighted the name "Paul Bunyan." In the depths of the Great Depression he was looking for ways of creating business for his shop. The printer's name was Merrill Cragun, father of Dutch!

Craguns had the first motel type unit as a resort in Minnesota.

Merrill Cragun next organized the Paul Bunyan Playground Association as a way of developing a theme for promoting resort business in northern Minnesota. At that time the State of Minnesota had only a one person Department of Tourism; that person was Ruth Abel and her efforts were pretty much limited to distributing brochures in the state capitol. There was a slow but steady response to Cragun's efforts and it resulted in more printing for his shop (located in the Midway District of Minneapolis and St. Paul). He designed and printed postcards with a Paul Bunyan theme, authored booklets of the delightfully exaggerated tales of the lumberjack and his men and even created a Paul Bunyan board game.

Merrill's wife, Louise helped create a demand for the game by calling on department stores and inquiring if they had the game in stock!

A significant breakthrough occurred in 1935 when Cragun was successful in convincing the Brainerd Chamber of Commerce to hold a Paul Bunyan festival – including a gigantic parade, a play about Paul's life, fireworks, log rolling and other festivities. There was also a beard-growing contest. And woe to the Brainerd man who did not grow a beard; he was hauled into a kangaroo court and fined accordingly. The characters who played Paul Bunyan and his men walked on stilts and swung huge ax-heads on ropes as they led the parade. Roy Wicklund, the operator of a small Brainerd grocery store, played the part of Paul and became somewhat of a local hero. He ran for Crow Wing County sheriff and won, serving several terms thereafter.

Cragun even convinced a local garment manufacturer, Les Hickerson, to create Paul Bunyan jackets made of red and black plaid. Cragun received a one cent royalty on every jacket sold!

The Chamber of Commerce reaped over $300 in profits that first year and for awhile thereafter produced Paul Bunyan events annually. However, in 1937 the chamber executive allegedly absconded with the entire treasury. About that time a twin cities' sculptor approached the Brainerd chamber and offered to create statues of Paul and Babe (his Blue Ox), but, alas, there was no money. The sculptor went to Bemidji and there created the masterpiece still on display. Reportedly the cost was only slightly over $300!

Cragun and his college buddy, Jack Madden (founder of Madden's Resort and Conference Center) earned some cash during the Paul Bunyan festivals by operating a hamburger stand by the old Crow Wing County jail building[2] in downtown Brainerd. They called their sandwich a "Wimpy-burger", named for a character in the Popeye comic strip, Wimpy, who loved hamburgers.

Meanwhile, the Paul Bunyan Playground Association grew and prospered, with Jack Madden as its president and Merrill Cragun as the treasurer. In 1943, most of the resorts in this organization surviving World War II formed the Minnesota Resort Association.

As mentioned earlier in this chapter, Jack Madden purchased a golf course in 1934 (now part of the Madden properties). He wanted to see resorts locate on the south end of Gull Lake to help provide golfers for his course. He encouraged his good friend Merrill Cragun to go into the resort business and brokered the sale of lakeshore property to him, and that was the beginning of the Cragun enterprises we know today. The Citizens State Bank of Brainerd financed the construction of eight cabins. The papers for the loan were signed on Saturday, December 6, 1941

– the day before the bombing of Pearl Harbor by the Japanese! The timing couldn't have been worse. With World War II in full swing there was little tourism in northern Minnesota. But the resort did open – a true "Ma and Pa" establishment.

Meanwhile, Cragun kept his twin cities shop going and even landed a contract to print labels for jars of Skippy Peanut butter – a GI favorite. On weekends, because of gas rationing, he would take the train to Brainerd, by way of Staples, usually carrying supplies for the resort with him – even food for the family. As a youngster, Dutch helped with the resort and at 8 years of age, was in charge of the bait business. Although Merrill was gone most of the time, he did serve as Civil Defense Warden for the area during the war.

With the end of the war, tourism in northern Minnesota really took-off. Merrill continued his printing business but with the end of gas rationing, drove to Gull Lake each weekend, pulling a small trailer behind him – full of all sorts of supplies for the resort. The Craguns kept adding cabins. Merrill's philosophy was "pay for your cabins, mortgage them, build more cabins, pay off the mortgage, borrow more money, build more cabins.... Dutch and Irma seem to have bought into the philosophy as this Ma and Pa resort has grown year by year into a huge resort and conference center including a lodge with over 300 rooms, an indoor pool, indoor and outdoor tennis courts and recreation centers, high tech conference rooms etc. Today it is among the largest in the Midwest.

Characteristic of their growth is the fact that in the early years Cragun's and the neighboring resorts shared a party line for telephone service. Today, Cragun's alone – with its huge lodge, several cabins, and multi conference facilities, has nearly 500 telephones! Their high tech conference facilities include the potential for satellite communications with the rest of the world. The carts on their golf course even have GPS instruments so that the golfers always know where the next hole is and how far, and course managers can keep track of the carts and possible problems.

Dutch and Irma believe that one of the most significant milestones in the development of their enterprise was when they became a year-round operation. The first winter they received some great publicity when Jim Klobuchar, former Minneapolis Tribune columnist, organized a group of 40 cross country skiers. They camped the first night on Rock Lake, near Pillager. Thirty-six below zero temperatures helped all of them to look forward to the second night at Cragun's. The extreme weather had frozen the facilities in all the cabins, but Dutch and his crew were successful in thawing out enough cabins to sleep everyone. Klobechar's columns reported the adventure as a very positive experience and gave the winter operations a real jump-start.

We began the Cragun story with the Paul Bunyan connection; we should conclude by reporting that Brainerd eventually acquired its own Paul Bunyan. Ray Bang and Sherm Levis, two visionary Brainerd businessmen, purchased the huge animated Paul Bunyan which had been featured in the Chicago Railroad Fair. It performs daily in the summer months at the Paul Bunyan Amusement Center in Baxter, at the intersection of highways 210 and 371.

Island View Lodge

Island View Lodge is now a part of Craguns; its well known restaurant has been renamed "the Hungry Gull."

The resort was founded by the Walter Framptons and sold to Ben and Eleanor Curry in 1945. Ben is one of the delightful legends of Gull Lake resort history. For example, he earned his instrument license as a pilot at age 72!

The resort was owned by Darrell and Sandy Bearson prior to being purchased by Cragun's.

Bar Harbor — old and new

Today, the *Bar Harbor Restaurant* is well known, but the original *Bar Harbor*, located across the highway on the channel to Lake Margaret, probably can be credited with first making Gull Lake so well known state-

Courtesy Crow Wing County Historical Society

The original Bar Harbor

wide. It was opened in 1938 under the management of Erv Anderson of Rocky Point — son of Charles Anderson, founder of the resort by that name. Erv's brothers, Herb and Art had some involvement but Herb was kept pretty busy at this time running the family resort and Art had other outside interests. It was a huge, barn-like building with an enormous dance floor, a long bar with service from both sides, a lounge with scores of slot machines and a room for high-stake gambling. Big bands, some well known, provided music for dancing. Celebrities came from as far away as Hollywood. Perhaps the best known patron was Clark Gable. Gable also fished and hunted on the lake and sometimes stayed at Breezy Point on Pelican Lake and Anderson's Rocky Point. At that time, other area nightclubs, such as *Deauville* (now Zorbaz) and the *Spotlight* provided ample opportunities for gambling, but Bar Harbor was the largest and best known.

This center for entertainment really flourished after World War II with the end of gas rationing and the return of GIs, but the era came to and end with the elections of 1946, when Luther Youngdahl became Governor of Minnesota. He decided to enforce the state's anti-gambling laws — and with a vengeance. As described earlier in this chapter in the piece about Grand View Lodge, Youngdahl was staying there when he saw first hand the gambling and accompanying "wild life" in the area. Places like Bar Harbor were soon out of business, and when it burned in 1958, it was never re-built.

Speaking of governors, Gull Lake was home to Governor C. Elmer Anderson and Governors Floyd Olson and Luther Youngdahl both had summer places on the lake.

When Anderson was governor, the state did not provide a mansion in St. Paul. Elmer and Lillian's home on the north end of Gull was therefore the official governor's mansion. A great deal of government business was transacted on the bench at the end of Anderson's dock! Mr. and Mrs. Hanspeter Borgwarth currently own the house and it is recognized as an historic site.

Gull Point was originally called Squaw Point. The name probably came from the large population of Ojibwe located in villages on both sides of the base of the point and also on both sides of Gull River where it leaves the lake. There has been some speculation that the name was given by lumberjacks who waved at the Indian women when they passed there on their log drives. In the 1990s, the state legislature passed a law banning the use of the word "squaw" to designate geographic locations. The law came about because the word is thought to have certain derogatory sexual connotations. Incidentally, this negative interpretation is still being debated by some language authorities.

Ron's Steak House on Gull Point is one of the older establishments on the lake and is a popular place for food and drink. The annual northern pike tournament (usually in August) is headquartered here.

More about names

Dutchman's Bluff at the northeast end of the lake gets its name from three men of Dutch descent who lived there at different times. They were Dutch Ludwig, Herman Roessner and Frederick "Fritz" Schultz. The latter served for many years as chief caretaker of Grand View Lodge. It was sometimes called Tower Hill, because of the forestry tower that was built in 1913. (A fire tower was built in the Pillsbury Forrest on the west side of the lake in 1912). As mentioned earlier, Dutchman's Bluff was the site of Curly Head's village.

Lutefisk Bay, running north from Gull (Squaw) Point, is so called because of all the Scandinavian families who built cabins there between World War I and II; most were from Brainerd.

Booming Out Bay at the north end near the channel to Upper Gull is named for the rafts of longs that were assembled there, held together by other logs, chained to each other, called booms. Thus it was possible to push or pull large numbers of logs across the lake to the Gull River outlet.

Pike Bay, located near the Gull-Round Lake thoroughfare, has two stories as to how it received its name: (1) it is named for the fish that abound there and (2) it is named for Rev. Pike who served for a time at the St. Columba Mission. It is also called Hole-in-the-Day Bay.

Ruth Lake was originally called School Section Lake. It was so called because in Minnesota, all sections numbered 16 and 36 were reserved for educational purposes. The lake is now named for Ruth White, whose family and relatives were early residents on the lake.

Cinosam Point is "Masonic" spelled backwards; some of the early residents were Masons.

Schaefer's Point is named for the Ted Schaefer family who had an early summer residence there. Schaefer had a meatmarket in downtown Brainerd on 6th street and his sons started the supermarket on Highway 371 near the lake.

Freeman Thorp and Clark Lake

In 1908, Freeman Thorp, a world renown painter of portraits of famous people, built a castle-like home on Lake Clark — then called "Upper Fishtrap." Here, he raised his family. When his invalid son, Clark, died in

The Thorp Castle on Clark Lake

1896 (and was buried here), Thorp persuaded the state to change the name of the lake from Upper Fishtrap to Clark, to honor his son.

Thorp was commissioned to paint seven presidents — from Lincoln to McKinley. Eight of his paintings are hanging (as of 1999) in the nation's capitol building, including Presidents Lincoln, Garfield and McKinley.

Thorp's daughter, Sarah, was also an artist of national stature; she used her married name, Sarah Heald. She also taught art in the Brainerd area. The author's father, Richard Lund, had some instruction from Mrs. Heald.

Footnotes

[1]Also called Hole-in-the-Day Bay.

[2]Now the site of the Crow Wing County Historical Society.

CHAPTER VIII

Things to See and Do in the Gull Lake Area*

Amusement, Attractions, Activities, Recreation, Theater, Museums

Brainerd Bowling Center & Scoreboard Sports Lounge, 301 Golf Course Road North, Baxter. Phone: 829-8899. Definitely a fun place to play...bowling, sports lounge, game room, snack bar. Home of Thunder Alley.

Brainerd Helicopter Service, Junction of Highways 371 and 210, Baxter. Phone: 829-5484. Located at Paul Bunyan Amusement Center. Helicopter rides daily.

Bump N' Putt Family Fun, Hwy. 371, Nisswa. Phone: 218-568-8833. Logger's Mini-Golf – The "Challenge" for young & old – Bumper Boats – Water Wars – Hoops! Basketball – young kids activities. Lots of space to enjoy. Hwy. 371 – 4 miles north of Nisswa.

Crow Wing County Historical Society, 320 Laurel Street, Brainerd. Phone: 829-3268, In the old Crow Wing County jailhouse. See an original jail cell and learn about the logging and railroad industries that built Crow Wing County. Open year round.

Kart Kountry, Highway 371, Brainerd. Phone: 829-4963. 4 miles N of Brainerd & ½ mile S of BIR on Hwy. 371. Go-karts for all ages on 3 tracks. 2 Mini-Golf courses, video arcade, batting cages & more.

Lakes Area Children's Museum, East Brainerd Mall, Highway 210, Brainerd. Phone: 825-0352. Children, ages 2 – 12, enjoy a variety of hands-on science and art activities. An indoor slide, a climbing complex and the KYDZ TV Studio add to the fun.

Nisswa Family Fun Center, County Road 77 and Highway 371, Nisswa. Phone: 963-3545. One admission price for unlimited water slides all day. New 1997 large-heated wading pool. Also rental roller blades & equipment to use on our ¼ mile track.

Paul Bunyan Amusement Center, Junction of Hwys. 210 and 371, Baxter. Phone: 829-6342 or 877-PBUNYAN. Unlimited enjoyment of over 30 rides

principal source – Brainerd Area Chamber of Commerce

& attractions for one low gate admission. Mini-golf, bumper boats, batting cage. Trampoline Thing and Space Probe are at extra charge. Animated Paul Bunyan.

Paul Bunyan Bowl, 1871 Excelsior Road North, Baxter. Phone: 829-3150. Automated scoring. Moonlight bowling on Saturday nights. Full bar. Video games. Pool. Pull tabs. Birthday parties.

Pirate's Cove Adventure Golf, 3995 Hwy. 371 N, Brainerd. Phone: 828-9002. Putt your way through mountain caves, over foot bridges & under waterfalls. Test your putting skills on 18 challenging holes of fun, excitement & thrilling pirate scenes.

Rolling Thunder, 1870 Highway 371 North, Brainerd. Phone: 825-0933. Super track for enjoying both CAM Cars and Nazcarts. Huge video arcade, vending machines and food. Fun for the whole family.

Ski Gull, County Road 77, Nisswa. Phone: 963-4353. Located on west side of Gull Lake. 14 runs. 20% advanced, 20% intermediate, 60% beginner, 1 triple chair & 3 rope tows. Downhill sledding. New rental equipment. Snowmaking. Lighted for night skiing. Chateau serving food & beverages.

This Old Farm Antique Museum & Old Time Village, 7344 Highway 18 East, Brainerd. Phone: 764-2915. Enjoy a day of fun. See 10,000 antiques on display. Log house, school house, sawmill, blacksmith shop & depot. All set up as it was years ago.

Bird Watching

Here are a few locations to note:

Eagles nests – Watch these national treasures feed their young! These eagles nests are located on Hwy. 371 just north of Nisswa, past the lake and bridge on the west side of the road. Nests are in the tops of the white pine trees throughout the area.

Heron Rookery – A blue heron rookery is located on County Road 77 (Pine Beach Road) just west of Madden's Resort. Watch these majestic birds from the roadside.

Northland Arboretum – Stroll through this area to see many varieties of birds as they fly from flower to flower & tree to tree.

Osprey nests – These birds are often mistaken for eagles. Their nests are located near Pillsbury State Forest west of Brainerd on Highway 210 and north on County Road 18 on the power line poles as well as other parts of the area.

Paul Bunyan Nature Learning Center – Quietly walk the trails and listen for the bird songs and don't forget your binoculars!

Casinos

Grand Casino Mille Lacs, Highway 169, Onamia. Phone: 320-532-7777 or 800-626-5825. Located on the west side of Mille Lacs Lake on Highway 169. All new Kid's Quest and video arcade. Over 1200 video slots. 36 blackjack tables. 5 great restaurants. Bingo. Gift shop. Valet parking.

Northern Lights Casino, Junction of Highway 371 and 200, Walker. Phone: 218-547-2744 or 800-252-PLAY. Slots. Video Poker, Keno, Progressives, Live Blackjack, 24 hour restaurant and full service bar. – Open 7 days a week.

Cruises

The Knotty Bear, Gull Lake, Brainerd. Phone: 828-8444. Begin your northern Minnesota memory with a narrated tour of beautiful Gull Lake. Enjoy a romantic evening dinner cruise or an afternoon lunch or cocktail cruise.

Laughing Loon at Driftwood Resort, Whitefish Lake, Pine River. Phone: 218-568-4221. 65 ft. true paddlewheel. Up to 60 passengers. Cruises on the Whitefish Chain. Also dinner cruises. Reasonable rates. Call for reservations.

Duck and Turtle Races

Duck Races – Pine River. Held every Friday mid-June – mid-August at 1 p.m. Phone: 218-587-4000 or 800-728-6926.

Turtle Races – June-August every Wednesday at 2 p.m. in downtown Nisswa. Bring your own turtle or borrow one for $1. Phone: 963-2620.

Golf Courses

Birch Bay Golf Course, County Road 77, Nisswa. Phone: 963-4488 or 800-450-4481. E-mail: baybox@brainerd.net. Nine holes par 36. Mature trees. Fun & challenging layout. Early bird and twilight rates daily. Free baby-sitting, free beginner lesson. Senior & family programs. Lakefront lodging on site. Since 1958.

The Traditional Course, Breezy Point Resort, County Road 11, Pequot Lakes. Phone: 218-532-7177 or 800-950-4961. "Shotmakers" course that rewards accuracy over power and is enjoyed by golfers of all abilities. Challenging golfers since the 1920's.

The Classic, Madden's Resort, County Road 11, Brainerd. Phone: 829-2811 or 800-642=5363. Rated 3rd Best New Upscale Public Course in North America by Golf Digest. Five sets of tees will give golfers the option of playing from 4,883 yards to 7,109 yards. Restaurant.

Craguns Robert Trent Jones II Courses, at the intersection of Highways 77 and 70, seven miles west of Highway 371. 45 holes (two 18 hole and a reversible 9 hole Irons course) in a spectacular setting; achieving International Audobon Signature Sanctuary status for minimalist design, by retaining and preserving the environment. Also featured practice facility staffed with P.G.A. pros plus a learning academy for all levels of golf. Large club house has restaurant and event facilities for club members, resort guests and the public.

The Garden Course, Grand View Lodge, County Road 77, Nisswa. Phone: 963-3146 or 888-837-4637. A 9-hole, par 35 course known for its spectacular scenery and colorful flowered fairways. Often called "The best kept secret in Minnesota."

Irish Hills Golf Course, County Road 44, Pine River. Phone: 218-587-2300 or 888-835-2300. 18 holes, par 72, 6000 yards. The natural surroundings of the Whitefish Chain of Lakes, makes Irish Hills an enjoyable golf course for all levels of golfers.

Madden's Pine Beach East, County Road 77, Brainerd. Phone: 829-2811 or 800-642-5363. Features one of the country's only par 6's! Twilight fees after 3 p.m.

Madden's Pine Beach West, County Road 77, Brainerd. Phone: 829-2811 or 800-642-5363. Heavily wooded course with rolling terrain – twilight greens fees after 3 p.m.

Pine Meadows, 500 Golf Course Drive, Baxter. Phone: 829-5733 or 800-368-2048. Located behind Mills Fleet Farm in Baxter. 18 holes (semi-private), par 72, 6,372 yards.

Pine Ridge Golf Club, Highway 10, Motley. Phone: 218-575-3300. Beautiful rolling hills 18 hole course. Par 73, 6,100 yard public course. Great food & your favorite cocktails.

Pine River Country Club, County Road 2, Pine River. Phone: 218-587-4774. Located 30 miles North of Brainerd on Highway 371. Beautiful 9 hole golf course. Located in jack pine woods. Open to the public.

Ruttger's Bay Lake Lodge Golf, County Road 6, Deerwood. Phone: 218-678-2885 or 800-450-4545. Located 5 miles north of County Road 18. The Lakes 18-hole championship and Alec's Nine golf courses. New clubhouse and restaurant. Original Ruttger's Resort; oldest resort under continuous family management in Minnesota.

The Pines, Grand View Lodge, County Road 77, Nisswa. Phone: 963-3146 or 888-837-4637. Soft rolling hills and prime Minnesota forests. Nationally recognized for its 27 championship holes. Natural hazards and multiple tees on every hole make course scenic & challenging. Large driving range, practice areas, putting green.

The Preserve, Grand View Lodge, County Road 107, Pequot Lakes. Phone: 963-3146 or 888-837-4637. A unique and distinctive golf opportunity awaits you. 240 acres, features bent grass throughout, 12 elevated tees through birch woods and 40 acres of wetland. Clubhouse with casual dining & a spectacular view of the course.

The Vintage at Staples, Staples. Phone: 218-894-9907. Nestled along the Crow Wing River. 25 minutes West of Brainerd. The Vintage provides golfers with 18 championship holes. The 6,600 yard public course is carved from 269 acres of scenic forest and features a slope rating of 130 from the blue tees.

Whitebirch Golf Course, Breezy Point Resort, County Road 11, Pequot Lakes. Phone: 218-532-7177 or 800-950-4960. Over 6,700 yards of lush fairways, fast undulating greens, sand, water & woods, range, pro shop and electric carts. Special midweek & twilight rates after 3:00 p.m. 9 hole golf & dinner package after 5:30 p.m. weekdays.

Whitefish Golf Club, County Road 16, Pequot Lakes. Phone: 218-543-4900. One of the most scenic and sought after courses to play in the Brainerd Lakes Area. Whitefish offers outstanding golf at a reasonable price. Whitefish golf....simply a matter of course!

Parks, Picnic Areas and Public Beaches

Crow Wing State Park – Phone: 829-8022. 9 miles south of Brainerd on Highway 371, at the confluence of the Crow Wing & Mississippi Rivers. 18 miles of hiking trails, tour the historic Crow Wing townsite and canoe the scenic rivers. MN state park vehicle permits required.

Deep Portage Conservation Center – Phone: 218-682-2325. North of Pine River just off Highway 84. Workshops, field activities, lecture demonstrations & classes on a wide variety of topics. Cross-country & hiking trails, snowmobiling, snow shoeing & hunting.

Gull Lake Federal Army Corp. Of Engineers – Phone: 829-3334. Located north on Highway 371 to County Road 125 (Gull Lake Dam Road) at Gull Lake. Shaded picnic area, grills, shelter, fishing bridge, playground & sandy beach. Boat launch. Small fee required. Beach closes at 10 p.m. and no life guard on duty.

Lum Park – On Rice Lake 1 mile East of the East Brainerd Mall, Brainerd. Swimming beach, shelters, playground, fishing dock. Public launch.

Northland Arboretum – Phone: 829-8770. In Brainerd west on Highway 210 north on NW 7th Street (north of Westgate Mall). Open all year from 8 a.m. – until dark. 500 acres of preserved land & wildlife to view and enjoy. 30 acre plant collection with 12 miles of hiking trails. Unpaved bike trails & lighted cross country ski trails during the winter.

North Long Lake – On Highway 371 North 7 miles north of Brainerd. Swimming, boat launch, picnic area. No life guard.

Paul Bunyan Nature Learning Center – Phone: 829-9620. 3 miles north on Highway 371 to County Road 49 East. Hiking trails, interpretive programs, workshops and nature related activities. Open year around and hours vary by season. Many programs are free.

Pillsbury State Forest – Phone: 828-2565. 8 miles west of Brainerd on Highway 210. Hiking and horse trails, picnic areas, shelter, boat launch, swimming.

Paul Bunyan State Trail

A 100 mile all-season recreational trail. 50 miles of paved trail surface 10 to 12 feet wide starting in Baxter & continuing to Hackensack.* Travels through six communities, along 21 lakes, crosses nine rivers and streams & cuts through pristine pine forests and wild wetlands.

Open year-around. Snowmobile use (metal studs are restricted) in the winter and non-motorized use the remainder of the year. Designed for hikers, skaters & bicyclist of all ages and abilities. Handicapped accessible.

Bunyan Trail Mileage – community to community:

Baxter/Brainerd to Merrifield . . . . .9 miles

Merrifield to Nisswa . . . . .7 miles

Nisswa to Pequot Lakes . . . . .6 miles

Pequot Lakes to Jenkins . . . . .3 miles

Jenkins to Pine River . . . . .6 miles

Pine River to Backus . . . . .8.8 miles

Backus to Hackensack . . . . .7 miles

Parking Lots Along the Trail:

Baxter: On Excelsior Street behind Westgate Mall

Merrifield: Use public access on North Long Lake

Nisswa: Parking lot behind Triangle Oil/76 Station

Pequot Lakes: Parking lot along trail in downtown

Pine River: Parking lot along the trail

Jenkins: Off-street parking

Backus: Parking lot along the trail

Hackensack: Parking lot along the trail

---

* There are plans to extend the trail farther north at this writing (1999).

Public Restrooms on the Trail:

Merrifield: Across Highway 25 at Merrifield Lions Park & satellites at the public access on North Long Lake.

Nisswa: Chamber building on the trail.

Pequot Lakes: In Chamber building during office hours.

Jenkins: Public restrooms east of trail on north side of town in City Park.

Hackensack: Public restrooms on the trail.

Seasonal Satellite Restrooms:

In the parking lots of Baxter, Nisswa and Pequot Lakes.

Race Tracks

Brainerd International Raceway, Hwy. 371 N. Brainerd. Phone: 612-475-1500, Minneapolis. Located 6 miles N. of Brainerd on Hwy. 371. See some of the top name drivers in the nation. NHRA professional Drag Racing, AMA National Motorcycle Racing & Street Rod/Street Machine events. Advance sale tickets are available.

North Central Motor Speedway, Hwy. 371 S, Brainerd. Phone: 828-1545. 5 miles S. of Brainerd on Hwy. 371. Racing every Saturday. Hot-laps at 7 p.m. Races at 7:30 p.m. Wissota Modified, Superstocks & Street Stocks, NCMS Pure-Stocks.

Riding Stables

Outback Trail Rides, Highway 210, Pillager. Phone: 746-3990. Boarding, training & trail ride facility. Trail rides range from one hour to full day rides into Pillsbury State Forest. Located 10 miles west of Brainerd on Hwy. 210. See you on the trail!

Whispering Pines Riding Stable, LLP, County Road 11, Crosby. Phone: 218-562-4377. One hour guided trail rides. Located 6 miles west of MN Highway 6 on County Road 11 or 5 miles east of County Road 3 on County Road 11.

Tennis Courts

Baxter Park – Located 2 miles west of Highway 371 & 210 intersection on Highway 210 W in Baxter. Two courts available.

Cragun's Indoor Courts – Pine Beach Road, south end of Gull Lake. Phone: 829-3591 ext 807. 2 indoor courts for rent, 6 outdoor courts.

City of East Gull Lake – Located near the Gull Lake Dam, off Gull Lake Dam Road. 2 courts available.

Gregory Park – 5th Street North, Brainerd. Located 2 blocks north of Washington Street. 5 courts available daily with lights available for night tennis.

Theater Productions

Central Lakes College – College Drive, Brainerd Community theater with numerous productions throughout the year from "Geritol Frolics" to the children's productions. Phone: 828-2521 for box office or 828-2589 for more information. Box office open noon-4:00 p.m.

Restaurants

Antlers, Breezy Point Resort, Pequot Lakes. Phone 218-562-7162. Serving lunch & dinner 7 days a week year round, in a spectacular setting, serving steaks, seafood & pasta. Lounge features specialty beers on tap.

Adirondack Coffee Specialties, Inc., 538 Main Street, Nisswa. Phone: 963-321. Espresso bar, casual gourmet dining in an Adirondack lodge setting.

Bar Harbor Supper Club, 6512 Interlachen Road, Gull Lake, Lake Shore. Phone: 963-2568. Casual dining with a lake side view. Steaks & broiled seafood. Live entertainment.

Black Bear Lodge & Saloon, Highway 371 North, Baxter. Phone: 828-8400. Three unique menus to choose from: All-you-can-eat Prime Rib Loft, Dinner Club menu and bar menu, all served in a northwoods log atmosphere. Full service bar open until 1 am. Serving lunch & dinner daily plus Sunday brunch.

The Classic Grill, Maddens Classic Golf Course, 8001 Pine Beach Peninsula, Brainerd. Phone: 829-2811. Sandwiches, salads and full cocktail service available.

Driftwood Family Resort & Golf, West end of Whitefish Chain, Pine River. Phone: 218-568-4221. A Scandinavian Smorgasbord and live Scandinavian music on Friday nights.

The Hungry Gull Restaurant & Rookery Bar, Cragun's Resort, 2001 Pine Beach Road, Brainerd. Phone: 829-3591. Exceptional fine dining in a beautiful northwoods setting, overlooking Gull Lake. Please call for reservations.

Italian Gardens, Grand View Lodge, S. 134 Nokomis, Nisswa. Phone: 963-2234. In the gardens of Grand View Lodge, you'll find a magical little cottage. Inside you'll be warmed by the rich aroma of authentic Italian cruisine. Family style.

Iven's On The Bay, 5195 North Highway 371, Brainerd. Phone: 829-9872. Fine seafood, casual dining at lakeside setting. Voted winner of "Best Food" by Lake Country Journal readers. Open daily 5:00 p.m. year round.

Kavanaugh's Resort & Restaurant, 2300 Kavanaugh Drive SW, Brainerd. Phone: 829-5226. A family owned resort with highly rated restaurant. Restaurant open to the public from Memorial weekend to Labor Day weekend.

Kelly's 10111 County Road 77 W. Nisswa. Phone: 828-4221. Located on the Pine Beach Rd (Cty 77) near Ski Gull. Casual & fun dining. Full American menu, Mexican specialties & homemade pizza. Full liquor service. Open 7 days a week. Serving lunch & dinner.

Lost Lake Lodge, 6415 Lost Lake Road, Lakeshore. Phone: 963-2681. www.lostlake.com. Fine Northwoods cuisine. The Lost Lake grist mill provides fresh stone ground flour for the breads served with every meal. Reservations required.

Madden's on Gull Lake, 8001 Pine Beach Peninsula, Brainerd. Phone: 829-2811. Patio and Bar Grill. Lobby Cafe. 19th Hole Lounge.

Marina Restaurant, Breezy Point Resort, Pelican Lake, Pequot Lakes. Phone: 218-562-7161. Lakeside dining, serving breakfast, lunch & dinner 7 days a week May-October, weekends – winter season. American cuisine, steaks, seafood, prime rib, Sunday brunch, live entertainment.

Morey's Market & Grille, Highway 371 North, Brainerd. Phone: 829-8248. Casual dining in a gourmet market setting. Wine, beer and espresso. Gourmet foods, cheese, sausage and ice cream. Gifts and "Up North" apparel.

Pauline's Restaurant & Saloon, 1851 Excelsior Road North, Baxter. Phone: 829-2318. Located next to Paul Bunyan Amusement Center. Casual dining with bar service. Lunch, dinner and Sunday breakfast buffet.

Quarterdeck Boathouse Restaurant on Gull Lake, 1588 Quarterdeck Road, Nisswa. Phone: 963-2482. Comfortable new theme restaurant.

Ron's Steak House, 1549 Gull Point Road NW, Gull Lake, Brainerd. Phone: 829-3918. Featuring seafood & all US Grade A Choice cuts of meat. Come by boat or car & dine in air conditioned comfort.

Ruttger's Bay Lake Lodge Restaurants, County Road 6, Deerwood. Phone: 218-678-2885. Located 5 miles north of County Road 18. Main Dining Room. Auntie M's Kaffeehouse and Zig's Steak & Pasta House.

Sherwood Forest Lodge, 7669 Interlachen Road, Nisswa. Phone: 963-2234 ext. 294. Nestled in the woods between Lake Margaret and Gull Lake.

Resorts and Conference Centers on the Gull Chain of Lakes*

Bay Colony Inn Resort and Reunion House

Nine units with sandy beach, level grounds, playground, game room, boats, catamarans, paddle boat, kids activities and Cable TV.
834 Gull Lake Drive, Nisswa, 56468; 218-963-2375; 800-843-1435.

Cold Spring Resort, Upper Gull Lake

Eleven units with lake-level cabins, complete kitchens with microwave, sandy beach, gameroom, playground, boat launching with plenty of dock space.
5168 County Rd. 29, Lake Shore, MN 56468; 218-568-5440.

Cragun's Resort and Conference Center

Two hundred and forty-eight units with TV, in-room movies, phone, marina, runabouts and pontoons for rent, new snowmobiles for rent, water-ski lessons, free children's program, indoor pool, sandy beach and indoor sports center. Full week, mid-week and weekend packages available. New golf course.
2001 Pine Beach Road, Brainerd, 56401; 218-829-3591; 800-272-4867; www.craguns.com

Grand View Lodge

One hundred and twenty-nine units with children's program, large tennis complex, two championship golf courses, nine-hole executive golf course, five restaurants, beautiful gardens and on National Register of Historic Places.
South 134 Nokomis, Nisswa, 56468; 218-963-2234; 800-432-3788.

Gull Bay Cabins

Three units; 218-963-7997; 800-900-7997; 924 Bishop Drive, Nisswa, 56468

Gull Four Seasons Resort

Thirty-one units including condos, chalets, cabins with complete kitchens, cable TV, spa, swimming pool, kiddie pool, boats, motors, pontoons, laundromat, playground and recreation room.
1336 St. Colombo Road, Brainerd, 56401; 218-963-7969; 800-964-4855; Email: vacation@gull4seasons.com; Web: www.gull4seasons.com.

Gull Lake Resort

Eighteen units with good elevation and sandy beach. New condos with dishwashers and stone fireplaces. All units have microwaves, color TV and cable TV.
1300 Gull River Lane NW, Brainerd, 56401; 218-829-1344; Web: www.gulllake.com.

---

* as reported by the chambers of commerce of the Brainerd Lakes area, unless otherwise designated, resorts are on Gull Lake proper.

Gull View Resort

Eight units with new Lund boat with each cabin, sleeper fish houses and snowmobile from cabin door.

2840 Van Sickle Bay Rd. West, Nisswa, 56468; 218-829-7464; 800-568-7376.

Lake Shore Bed and Breakfast on Upper Gull Lake

One-3 room suite with beach and view. Snowmobile from front door.

5210 Christy Drive, Lakeshore, 56468; 218-568-4450.

Lykins Pinehurst Resort

Nine units with beach, playground, basketball and volleyball.

7872 Interlachen Rd., Nisswa, 56468; 218-963-2485; 800-963-2485; Email: lykin@uslink.net.

Lost Lake Lodge on Lost Lake and Gull

Ten units on a private lake with kids programs. Rates include breakfasts and dinners.

6415 Lost Lake Rd., Lake Shore, 56468; 218-963-2681; 800-450-2681; Web: www.lostlake.com.

Madden's Resort and Conference Center

Two hundred and eighty-seven units with 63 holes of golf, kids' programs, restaurants, nightly entertainment, full marina and 3 sand beaches.

8001 Pine Beach Peninsula, Brainerd, 56401; 218-829-2811; 800-642-5363; Web: www.maddens.com; Email: maddens.com.

Manatauk Resort

Five units.

1094 Sandy Point Road; 219-963-4337; 800-842-8189; Email: efmelum@aol.com.

Nisswa Beach Resort

Opened in 1940 by George Lennow, a St. Paul entrepreneur who, among his other investments, owned Lexington Ball Park. Thyra Peterson managed the resort for over 40 years. Twelve units with screen porches, walking distance to town and close to bike trail.

P.O. Box 31, Nisswa, 56468; 218-963-2322; off season: 612-786-0028.

Point Narrows Resort on Bass and Upper Gull

Eight units with all lakefront cabins and gas at the dock. Seasonal camping sites.

5045 Point Narrows Rd., 218-568-5552.

Quarterdeck Resort and Boathouse Restaurant

Twenty-eight units with 2, 3 and 4 bedroom units. Eight villa rooms for couples.

1588 Quarterdeck Rd., Nisswa, 56468; 218-963-2482; 800-950-5596; Web: quarterdeckgulllake.com.

Rainbow Bay Resort on Margaret Lake

Nine Units.

6664 Rainbow Rd., Nisswa, 56468; 218-963-2302; 800-896-2302. Web: www.att.com.

Samara Point Resort

Seven units including deluxe homes with screen porches and fireplaces.

6161 Birchwood Hills Rd., Dept. BL98, Nisswa, 56468; 218-963-2615.

Sandy Beach Resort

Twenty-seven units with pontoon and motor rentals; spring and fall nightly rates.

7894 Sandy Point Rd., Nisswa, 56468.

Sorenson's Cabins

One unit; three rooms for two on the lake.

6522 Paine Ave. NW, Brainerd, 56401; 218-963-4333; 218-963-7410.

The Pointe Resort

Six units.

1593 Gull Point Rd., East Gull Lake, 56401; 218-829-2596; 800-950-2596.

Winter Sports

Snowmobiling and cross country skiing are popular and there are marked trails for both. The Paul Bunyan Trail may be accessed at the

Photo Courtesy George Cowie

The world's largest ice fishing contest draws participants from all over the nation, including Jeff Cowie on the far left from Phoenix, Arizona. Others are from the Twin City area; from left to right: Sue Berger, Jackie Anderson, Ed Anderson and Lynn Ulrich. Sponsored by the Jaycees annually in January.

north end of the lake. Rentals are available at places like Cragun's that are open year-around.

When traveling on the lake, it is important to follow marked trails and to stay away from any narrows — which always have thin ice and sometimes no ice at all.

Downhill skiing is available at Ski-Gull at the south end of the lake. Good slopes for beginners and intermediates, with two slopes for advanced. Many recent improvements.

We have already spoken about winter angling and spearing but we should mention the annual Jaycees ice fishing contest on Pike Bay at the north end of the lake; it is the nation's largest.

Fishing and Hunting

As we have said in the previous chapter, the early resorts were primarily hunting and fishing camps. Fish boat rentals were an important source of income. Over the years, priorities and interests have changed. Conferencing, along with family vacations, have the greatest economic impact. Golf is now the number one sport. Water activities, of course, remain popular — including water skiing, boating, swimming, scuba diving and snorkeling. All of the larger resorts have tennis courts. Everyone can enjoy the beauty of the lakes and forests.

Fishing and hunting are no longer the dominant activities. Yet, The Gull chain of lakes still provides excellent fishing, as the pictures on the following pages attest. Local guides report that Gull ranks among the best for lunker walleyes, as well as northern pike. There is also good fishing for bass and pan fish.

Efforts have been made to introduce several species of trout into the lake but they have not been successful.

A stringer of Gull Lake walleyes taken in the "good old days" when limits were a little more generous.

Courtesy Crow Wing County Historical Society

Jim Hess (Staples) and John Hassig (Brainerd) and a nice string of opening day walleyes.

Trophy northerns from yesteryear.

Courtesy Craguns.

Jack Nelson, Henning and John Hassig, Brainerd, with a nice string of "eaters" out of Gull Lake.

Guide Ray Gildow, Staples, with another nice Gull Lake walleye.

Bob Stericker, Staples, with a 22½ pound northern speared on Gull Lake.

Fishing guides are available through most resorts or through the Nisswa Guides Association. Marv Koep's Tackle Shop, Nisswa, is a good place to find a reliable guide.

The Gull Chain of lakes are popular for winter angling and spearing. House rentals are available through some resorts.

As mentioned earlier, the "world's largest" ice fishing contest is held annually on Pike Bay, also called Hole-in-the-Day Bay. There is also a summer northern pike contest based at Ron's Steak House on Gull Point.

Gull, at one time, was an excellent duck hunting lake for "divers". Bluebills (scaup) still visit the lake in large numbers just before freeze-up.

There is a good population of whitetail deer in the area and a fairly large amount of state land is still available for public hunting. There is also good grouse cover.

What of the Future?

It has been estimated that on any one summer day there are approximately 10,000 people on the Gull Lake Chain who can look out the windows of homes, cabins, restaurants, resorts or conference centers and see water. There are many thousands more who live on the rings of roads encircling the lakes who have ready access to them. Is Gull Lake in danger?

With so many people and increasing numbers each year, there surely are problems which much be recognized and dealt with if the excellent quality of life around the lake is to be continued. Fortunately, the community, township and county governments involved have demonstrated that they care very much about the lake and its resources. As corporate sewer systems replace septic tanks and zoning regulations are honored, we can be optimistic about the lake's future. The quality of water is probably better now than several decades ago. With reasonable care, future generations should be able to enjoy this great body of water and the associated chain of lakes as much as we do.

But . . . . *THE FUTURE OF GULL LAKE IS TRULY IN OUR HANDS.*

Suggested Further Readings

BY DR. DUANE R. LUND:
Andrew, Youngest Lumberjack
Our Historic Upper Mississippi
White Indian Boy
The Indian Wars

BY CARL ZAPFFE:
The Man who Lived in Three Centuries
Indian Days
Oldtimers
Oldtimers II

Other Books by Duane R. Lund
A Beginner's Guide to Hunting and Trapping
A Kid's Guidebook to Fishing Secrets
Fishing and Hunting Stories from The Lake of the Woods
Andrew, Youngest Lumberjack
The Youngest Voyageur
White Indian Boy
Lake of the Woods, Yesterday and Today, Vol. 1
Lake of the Woods, Earliest Accounts, Vol. 2
Leech Lake, Yesterday and Today
The North Shore of Lake Superior, Yesterday and Today
Our Historic Boundary Waters
Our Historic Upper Mississippi
Tales of Four Lakes and a River
The Indian Wars
101 Favorite Freshwater Fish Recipes
101 Favorite Wild Rice Recipes
101 Favorite Mushroom Recipes
150 Ways to Enjoy Potatoes
Camp Cooking, Made Easy and Fun
Cooking Minnesotan, yoo-betcha!
Early Native American Recipes and Remedies
Entertainment Helpers, Quick and Easy
Gourmet Freshwater Fish Recipes
Nature's Bounty for Your Table
Sauces, Seasonings and Marinades for Fish and Wild Game
The Scandinavian Cookbook
The Soup Cookbook
Traditional Holiday Ethnic Recipes - collected all over the world
101 Ways to Add to Your Income
Now That You Have Found It (For the New Christian)
Lessons in Leadership, Mostly Learned the Hard Way

About the Author

- EDUCATOR (RETIRED, SUPERINTENDENT OF SCHOOLS, STAPLES, MINNESOTA);
- HISTORIAN (PAST MEMBER OF EXECUTIVE BOARD, MINNESOTA HISTORICAL SOCIETY); Past Member of BWCA and National Wilderness Trails Advisory Committees;
- SENIOR CONSULTANT to the Blandin Foundation
- WILDLIFE ARTIST, OUTDOORSMAN.